Cowley Publications is a ministry of the brothers of the Society of Saint John the Evangelist, a monastic order in the Episcopal Church. Our mission is to provide books and resources for those seeking spiritual and theological formation. Cowley Publications is committed to developing a new generation of writers and teachers who will encourage people to think and pray in new ways about spirituality, reconciliation, and the future.

Praise for *The Play of Light*

"In lucid and lyrical prose, Lou Masson takes the seemingly insignificant details of daily life, the seemingly insignificant objects and experiences of memory, the brief words and gestures that linger, links them, transforms them, honors and reveals them to be the vital essence of existence. In *The Play of Light,* Masson demonstrates a manner, a way of observing that lifts the ordinary into the rare. This collection of essays itself is no ordinary gift but a rare one."

—Pattiann Rogers, author, *Firekeeper: Selected Poems*

"*The Play of Light* is one of those beautifully quiet books that takes hold of the reader—the reader's heart—the way a clear gathering of stars can, nudging him to wonder . . . to remember. The poetry and grace found in ordinary moments, nourished by memory, by the human spirit open to connecting, accepting, become extraordinary in Lou Masson's admirable mission; reading his bright, loving meditations on the everyday miracles he has carried forward—the kind of miracles we all carry and, if we pause just long enough, can feel again—was an experience of pure joy."

—Gary Gildner, author, *Somewhere Geese are Flying*

"Louis Masson considers everyday moments in an ordinary life, turning them this way and that until a certain play of light reveals in them something blessed and extraordinary. The elegance of his language, and the gracefulness of his thought, elevate these reflections, these prose poems, to the level of prayer—gentle, irresistible, quietly satisfying prayers of a wise heart."

—Molly Gloss, author, *The Jump-Off Creek,*
The Dazzle of Day, and *Wild Life*

"Lou Masson attends with care to the natural world and to daily human concerns so that again and again, expectation yields to surprise. In the rich sphagnum of narrative and detail, of anticipation and memory, lyrical insights are revealed. We feel the discoveries as our own, a testimony to Masson's elegant and understated prose. Writing as teacher, father, son, husband, and singular human being, Masson is unafraid to show us the intersections between doubt and hope."

—Michele Glazer, author, *Aggregate of Disturbances: Poems*

The Play of Light

*Observations and Epiphanies
in the Everyday World*

Louis J. Masson

Cowley Publications
CAMBRIDGE, MASSACHUSETTS

Published in the United States of America by Cowley Publications, a division of the Society of Saint John the Evangelist. No portion of this book may be reproduced, stored in or introduced into a retrieval system, or transmitted, in any form or by any means—including photocopying—without the prior written permission of Cowley Publications, except in the case of brief quotations embedded in critical articles and reviews.

Library of Congress Cataloging-in-Publication Data

Masson, Louis J., 1942–
The play of light : observations and epiphanies in the everyday world /
    Louis J. Masson.
        p. cm.
    Includes bibliographical references.
    ISBN 1-56101-240-8 (pbk. : alk. paper) 1. Meditations.
2. Masson, Louis J., 1942– I. Title.
    BX2182.3.M37 2005
    242—dc22

                                                    2005019392

ISBN-10: 1-56101-240-8
ISBN-13: 978-1-56101-240-4

Cover design: Brad Norr Design
Cover photo: Chris Highland, www.naturetemple.net
Interior design: Wendy Holdman

This book was printed in the United States of America
on acid-free paper.

Cowley Publications
4 Brattle Street
Cambridge, Massachusetts 02138
800-225-1534 • www.cowley.org

In memory of my parents, Louis and Evelyn,
who gave me the world, and for my grandson, Jackson,
who just discovered it

———

"The world is charged with the grandeur of God."
GERARD MANLEY HOPKINS

"He wore the world for wedding band."
DANIEL BERRIGAN

Contents

Epiphanies: A Prologue

> Then, opening their treasures, they offered him gifts of
> gold and frankincense and myrrh.
>
> MATTHEW: 2:11, 12

F IRST, A STORY. I was born in a rural Massachusetts
town a week after the Feast of the Epiphany on the
night of a severe winter storm. Neither the feast nor the
word *epiphany* held any special significance until the year
after I made my First Communion. Again it was a cold
year, one of several in a row, and I had been sick often,
often enough that I had to repeat a year. Those were still
the days of family doctors who made house calls, and our
doctor told my mother three warm meals a day would
help me to regain my strength.

So my mother prevailed on the Sister Superior of my
school, a nun both wise and kind, who offered to allow
me a warm lunch in the convent kitchen since it was too
far for me to walk or even take a bus home in the lunch
hour.

I sat at a little wooden table by the door, and I was the
ward of the cook, Sister Elizabeth, who, I fear, became
cook because she was not skilled enough to teach. From
the grumbles I often heard, she was not even an especially

good cook. The nuns, Sisters of the Holy Ghost, were from France and Canada, French speaking, and I greeted them in French as they arrived from their classes. Sister Elizabeth had coached me in conversational French. As Sister Elizabeth served, I heard through the door that swung open with her coming and going the Sisters at grace and the reading of the day, both in French.

It was Sister Elizabeth who told me that on the Feast of the Epiphany or on a day near it, her community celebrated with a cake in which was placed a pea, an Epiphany Pea. Whoever found the pea was prince and regarded as especially blessed that day. I could hear the Sisters at their cake and the lamentations and protest when no pea was discovered. My French was not good enough to understand the fine points of the commotion, but the tone in which Sister Elizabeth's name was repeated and the final stern raised voice of Mother Superior made it plain that Sister Elizabeth stood accused of gross incompetence. The Sisters returned to the school not entirely refreshed by their lunch. Some muttered as they draped their heavy woolen capes over their shoulders.

I prepared to leave also, to walk the short distance from convent to school. I wrapped my scarf around my neck and pulled down my watch cap. As she held the door open for me, Sister Elizabeth handed me a folded napkin that I unfolded as I walked through the long back porch where the Sisters hung their laundry, most likely washed by Sister Elizabeth. The napkin held a thin slice of cake, and in the slice the Epiphany Pea. I was prince. I looked back at Sister Elizabeth, and her homely and simple face broke into a maternal smile. Around her the long white habits drying on the clothesline fluttered like a host of angels. And that is how I remember Sister Elizabeth, smiling, clutching to her breast the silver dove that her order wore on a ribbon around their necks.

Snow crunched under my boots, the cold pinched my nostrils, gleaming light bejeweled the drifts of snow. The world was there to see, and for a few brief moments I looked deeply and saw what the Jesuit poet Gerard Manley Hopkins called "God's Grandeur."

I wish that I could say Sister Elizabeth remained in my life, but by giving me strength she guaranteed our separation, the loss perhaps, of the only child she would ever teach. I would see her sometimes on the porch hanging clothes and would wave to her. And then she disappeared, and I grew up, letting her memory fade among things left in childhood.

Years later, as a student at a Jesuit college, I learned that the Jesuit-trained Irish writer James Joyce used the term *epiphany* to describe flashes of insight where a character or reader suddenly has a realization. And reading his stories returned me to the porch where Sister Elizabeth stood among the laundry that moved in the breeze like angels. She could have walked out of a Joyce story. And in remembering her, I had my epiphany about what I might have meant to her—a sweet, simple, homely, and, I fear, lonely woman who humbly served her God.

I remembered too the pea, a little bit of nothing really, that allowed me to see the world aglow. In the last lines of his poem "God's Grandeur," a poem that celebrates the spiritual that charges our everyday world, Father Hopkins takes comfort

Because the Holy Ghost over the bent
World broods with warm breast and with ah!
bright wings.

Reading the lines, I am again the boy prince, and behind me Sister clutches her silver dove. And it was and is so ordinary. Yet it was extraordinary, too. I suspect we all have been led to that spiritually charged world by some back door. And we have carried a simple key to its mysteries given to us by someone who loved us. Who has not seen the snow glisten, seen the saintly in the humble, the story in the wordless exchange of two people? We all carry the epiphany pea in our pocket, and every life has its moments of revelation. What follows is the play of memory and epiphany in a rather ordinary life spent with family, in the classroom, in church, among books, and in nature—the commonplace revelations of the Holy Ghost's bright wings that can draw from us, like Hopkins, the exclamation: "Ah!"

The Play of Light

I

To Catch All the Days:
Epiphanies of Nature

Gentle Rain from Heaven

O VER AND OVER we gently edit the rough draft of memory into an orderly narrative that we see as our life. For most of us it is an ongoing and unpublished narrative. The thought of all the unpublished pages that I have accumulated intrigues me as I realize that my next decade will bring me to a biblical three score and ten years. Today the calendar nears the end of spring, when summer has already taken possession and the world seems new again. I sit in a corner of my bedroom bent over a small table, facing shelves of books. Behind me my bed; next to me a window that looks out over the porch roof to linden trees. Already they wear their deepest green and sport buds on narrow leaf-like blades that, come fall, will whirl about me like brown helicopters as I rake another summer into piles.

My world is at my fingertips: the room, merely a couple of steps away from my family; the bed, where my dreams and nightmares take me where they will; the books, windows to others' lives; and my own window, opening on the world of nature. But I have yet to rake these intersecting realms into their own piles. Where to begin? Under this summer sun, the out-of-doors pulses in marvelous confusion all around me. But this summer is the child of spring, and spring the child of winter rain. Begin with rain:

Rain, rain, go away. I remember the days before Christmas. *Come again some other day . . .* The old chant came unbidden as I endured another shower or driving storm. If who we are is determined in part by where we are, then rain begets much in the character of an Oregonian, even a transplanted one like myself.

This Christmas season I wound my way up the hills that rise in the west above the Willamette River. I was on my annual hunt for the cut-your-own Christmas tree; in our family tradition, already-cut trees from lots are a taboo. Although as the cutter and primary hauler of our Christmas trees, I have honored the tradition grudgingly.

There's no snow at the crest of the hills, but there are puddles galore. I trudged further and further away from the pickup where the owner of the tree farm waited with his wife and daughter, the truck engine running to take the chill out of the cab, Christmas carols blaring from the dashboard radio. Just before I found the perfect tree, a mist infiltrated the Douglas firs and fogged my glasses. I took off my spectacles and let cool fingers of mist caress my face. The mist became gentle rain, and it lifted and wafted among the smell of loam and fir needles, the odor and taste of the green and wet Northwest.

As I drove down the hill with tree lashed atop my van, my arms and back ached from unaccustomed exertion—this annual adventure is the closest I come to being a logger. I thought of mythic Oregon, the aggressively verdant place that a young Ken Kesey captured, three decades ago, in perhaps the most accomplished literary homage to the region and its hardiest denizens. *"Look,"* says Kesey in the first pages of his novel *Sometimes a Great Notion,* and immediately we are seeing his world through a veil of rain, and rain is the curtain that closes the 600-page saga. Rain is very nearly a character in Kesey's story, and rightly so. He merely puts on paper what any Northwesterner feels to be true. We love and sometimes endure our rain as we might a sibling or parent or spouse, for better or for worse. And it falls on us all: writers, loggers, students, and middle-aged fathers hauling Christmas trees through the mist.

Look, I thought, once I was back down on level ground and looked back at the hills that reach into the valleys like armies on the move. The tree farm was shrouded in clouds, the very mists that had caressed my face. All was green, thick, and growing, but our rain forest is not lush or tropical; our woods are hard, a cold and patient evergreen nurtured by rain.

Live long enough in the Northwest and its rain will school you in patience and endurance. Northwesterners have convinced themselves, and anyone else who will listen, that they toil and suffer under endlessly gray skies, a dank burden known to no other inhabitants on the globe. In late summer, for example, before soccer and football start up again with the school year, the favorite sport of native Northwesterners is the issuance of ominous warnings to newcomers about the coming rains—the endless, sunless days of winter and spring.

Yet in the bright days of summer I, like many natives, become a bit touchy when a dry spell runs on. And when the first fall showers strike the dry pavement, cleansing it like a steam iron on freshly laundered clothes, I am thrust into a Gene Kelly mood of *just singing in the rain*. The same feeling comes over me when late-winter rains fall over cherry blossoms and perfume the land with the first intimations of spring.

Such gentle and persistent rain reveals our best character—a people not so much hardened by endurance as softened by patience, an open-faced and relaxed people. I think "laid back" was how I found them when I came west in the early seventies. I note with an ironic smile that new age musicians' self-help relaxation CDs feature orchestration with ocean or raindrop sounds, nature's everyday background music in the Northwest.

When I came west, half my life ago, I kept hearing that Oregon was "God's country." A place close to God? A place especially blessed by God? The latter, I suspect; and here I reach back for words, lines of poetry actually, that were part of a long passage from Shakespeare that a Jesuit scholastic thought schoolboys like me ought to memorize:

> The quality of mercy is not strained;
> It droppeth as the gentle rain from heaven.

Decades later the lines remain unforgettable, perhaps because they were among the earliest I put to memory or perhaps because my younger self took Shakespeare quite literally. Rain fell not from the sky then but from heaven, and for me it continues to.

As the nineteenth century turned toward the twentieth, the Jesuit Father Hopkins, who was a teacher as well

The Play of Light

as a poet, ended a dark sonnet written in the grip of deep despair with the plea: *O thou lord of life, send my roots rain.* He prayed from the country of the soul as others—rain dancers and makers, medicine men and priests—have ever prayed from the living earth to the heavens above: *God give us life; God send us rain.* And as the twentieth century turned toward the twenty-first, I gazed across a land nurtured by rain that certainly must fall as the blessings of answered prayers.

Puddle Wonderful

WINTER PASSED and in rain-washed air, I walked over, around, and through a day of puddles, each still and smooth as glass. Gray morning clouds dimmed the first light, and the puddles shone like shards broken and scattered from an immense mirror. Or perhaps they were the odd-shaped pieces of a jigsaw puzzle, tossed by a careless giant to tease my mind awake as I made my way across a parking lot.

A morning puddle under a gray sky catches reflections as if they were black and white photographs. Light painted nature's first pictures on water, and in some Eden another light must have aroused a consciousness in a body that shambled through a primal gallery. I too walk head down searching out the images at my feet, a vision of a world upside down. I look down at the tops of trees, odd corners of building roofs, even the hazy curves of clouds. Puddles everywhere and each one framing its own odd picture; it is a world that the poet e. e. cummings baptized "puddle-wonderful." It is a world seen through the eyes of children, or perhaps of an aging romantic like myself who has, since the days of remembered childhood, been a connoisseur of small bodies of water: drops, puddles, pools, and ponds.

Early on, my approach was more tactile. Puddles and ponds were made for walking through. Rainy days I leave that sort of thing to two little girls who live across the street from my home. The youngest, a redhead my family has nicknamed "Carrot Top," marches beneath a small umbrella in boots that climb almost to her knees in a ritual tromping through every puddle on her sidewalk. I estimate without any scientific survey but with great confidence that innumerable like-minded boys and girls are stomping puddles all over the city (perhaps all over the world where rain has fallen).

As I watch "Carrot Top," my toes remember the rubber against socks and how the cold felt wet even though the boots were waterproof, and the tension of being almost barefooted as the toes of the boots pushed against the resistance of the cold water.

My little neighbor goes from puddle to puddle peering into each image where up is now down, a looking glass world, a wonderland for an Alice on a rainy day. She puzzles over the images that she shatters and watches reappear. An act of destruction or creation? I guess both. There is a sense of power unchallenged by her parents: she can benignly break something. And then there is the magic of seeing it reappear perfectly intact each and every time. On to the next puddle. There is also the sound: the splash and plash against the boots and the delicious squishing of footfalls between puddles. Sometimes she stirs the upside-down world with a stick or her finger, chilled then to the second knuckle. And then on to the next puddle.

I envy her spontaneity, her delight in something so small, and recall my smallest memorable water-caught image. Once I stood between showers waiting for a bus. It was a makeshift stop mid-block where the just budding maples of the parking strip dipped their lowest branches to eye level. Slowly water gathered at the end of a bud in a large drop that plopped into a puddle at my feet. To pass the time, I counted the seconds it took for the drop to form and reach a weight that sent it falling. And as I watched, a small, dark nucleus formed in the middle of the drop. When I eyed it very closely just before it fell, I could see that it held a reflection of the tree that held it, but the tree upside down, a world caught in a drop of water.

That drop joining others followed the usual mathematics of puddles, but I have also watched them form by subtraction. A shallow meadow pond that grew larger with spring rain grew smaller and smaller in a very dry summer. In spring I searched it for frog jelly, and then the tadpoles that moved over the muddy bottom like animated commas and semicolons in their watery Eden. But as summer passed, the pond shrank and shrank until it was merely a large puddle, too small to hold the hundreds of frogs whose bright eyes protruded from the water and the ever-growing circle of mud. I have never seen such a concentration of frogs, nor of garter snakes that slithered from the dry grass to feast. In miniature here was the drama of a dying water hole with prey and predator playing traditional roles. Even in a small world, the old laws rule.

When I was a tadpole myself, I caught the wistful smile of my father watching me paddle in the icy pool of a creek

The Play of Light

or the warm shallows of a muddy pond. In time I would wear the same expression watching my own son taking his mark and leaping at the starter's signal into a chlorine pool. And I marked the line of my bones in his as he exploded over and into the water, taking me with him and leaving me behind. We travel into and beyond our life in water, growing in the liter or so of the womb, the puddle that holds and then precedes us into the world. This too is an old law.

I dipped my finger before a Mass into the holy water font at the door of the church. In his homily the priest spoke of the various blessings that may be performed by a priest, half joking that there was a book listing five thousand, covering all manner of creation. I thought of all the priests aspersing through time the world within their reach. I thought too of the rains from heaven that have fallen even before the old laws, leaving to this day myriad puddles as marks of grace.

Ponds

I THINK AGAIN of my little carrot-top neighbor with myriad puddles awaiting her bright red boots, and I wonder what she will remember when she outgrows her splashing days. On what pages of her memory will she record them? I find it impossible to journey back to my mind at her age. Too many memories intervene. And waking memory is not so unlike splashing a puddle whose reflections of the same object disjoin and reassemble in unpredictable ways. A memory I stir in summer shimmers in a cluster of stories about ponds. There are my memories and stories and those of my father, and they have melded together over time.

I suffered my first bout of homesickness at a summer camp, a non-fatal illness but for many of us a painful taste of the grief and loss that lie ahead. It was my intimation of mortality in a very bucolic and romantic setting. It was a Catholic camp by a lake, but it also had a small pond, perhaps spring fed, with a small island where there was a white marble statue of the Blessed Mother. At some point before my paid time was up, my parents came to rescue me, but before they did I remember retreating to the pond and watching the ghostly white reflection of Mary, whose extended arms seemed to beckon when a breeze or an irreverent frog rippled the dark mirror of water. Was I praying for rescue or looking for a place to cry unobserved or communing with the beauty of the scene? Looking back I have no idea, but that one memory remains from a summer that otherwise seems entirely forgotten. And over the years I've attached it to stories my father told.

My grandmother sent my father and my uncle to a seminary that began training young men in high school. My uncle was younger but left sooner; my father continued almost until ordination. Two seminary stories I know by heart. At the seminary there were two ponds, one very small and the other quite large, visited every year by a flock of mallards. In his description the small pond conformed in every detail to the pond of my homesickness. The small pond was the setting for the first story.

During an unstructured hour when they could be reading or writing home, two of the seminarians who hadn't quite mastered Christ's "turn the other cheek" over the years squared off against each other by the side of the small pool. In my father's telling, one of them was a huge fellow, a farm boy, and the other, a small wiry boy from a big city who had a cold mean streak. The bigger man was foot-slow but tall enough to protect his head, so the smaller fighter jabbed under his guard, striking the bigger boy's chest over the heart over and over until he crumbled, grasping for breath. Other seminarians circled them and shouted as men and boys will at a brawl. Before the standing fighter could move in to bloody his now vulnerable and beaten fellow seminarian, one of the deacons, who was quite an athlete and who would go on to be a missionary, broke the circle and shamed both the fighters and the watchers. In my father's telling everyone had a name, and in his memory a face and a life, details lost to me.

My father died many years ago. The circle of seminarians and the violence at that holy place now live only in my mind or in my telling. His memory has become my memory. And when I see the images of his story, the fight by the pond, it tends to merge with my pond. On the dark waters again I see the ghostly Mary whose hands tremble in the rippled reflection of the dark water.

A second story had to do with the larger pond and its mallards. My father told of the brother who cooked for the priest and the seminarians and who brought a bag of breadcrumbs and crusts to the pond every morning to feed the ducks. Since the brother usually presented a rather misanthropic face to the world, this St. Francis-like behavior remained a mystery. Then, on a day when the bishop was visiting the seminary, my father noticed that the brother returned from his morning charity to the ducks, grasping a still full bag. Small curled feathers decorated his shiny cassock. Apparently the bishop would dine on roast duck.

The summer before I turned sixty, I made a retreat with the Trappists. The abbey was backed by hills and opened on broad hay fields. A stream from the hills fed a series of ponds, quiet places to meditate or to watch the herons or deer or the nearly tame mallards, whose continuous quacks punctuated an otherwise silent community. As I walked around the edge of the pond, an ancient Trappist, wearing an orange watch cap even in mid-summer, limped to the pond where the mallards waddled to his sandaled feet. He tossed from a paper bag crusts and crumbs, pausing just long enough to smile before disappearing to whatever he did behind cloistered walls. My father's story seemed acted out, though the mallards were safe here among vegetarian monks. Their shed feathers floated on the reflection of the pond or settled into the prints left in the mud by the other creatures that shared the abbey grounds.

When I was a young boy growing up among Berkshire Hills, I sought out ponds where I scanned the mud for telltale tracks of raccoons and deer, and sometimes caught a muskrat off guard. I would frighten frogs whose sudden leaps and splashes would frighten me in turn. My days were free, so I could visit my ponds at odd hours when no one else would be about. Later in the year I might have encountered a hunter, but in the summer no one else seemed interested in the ponds I visited. I sat among wild iris and watched the wake of a swimming muskrat or concentrated for as long as it took to find the eyes of the bullfrog croaking among cattails. Often I would wait until the first lightning bug began to blink before I would reluctantly head home. It was not so many years before that I had cried by a pond to go home, and here I felt an ache to stay. Someday I told myself, I will buy land with a pond. Owning my own patch of scrub land with a little pond would make me a rich man indeed. I have yet to make the down payment.

Just as well perhaps, for what I wished to own was time linked to place, and neither was nor is really for sale. In one of his novels, the British writer John Fowles cautions that one cannot both love and possess. There is an inescapable truth in this warning. Maybe that is the ache of contemplating a pond when you are ten, or why an old Trappist monk smiles as he scatters breadcrumbs to a family of mallards.

Yet I would quibble with Fowles, pointing out the train tracks that ran along the embankment at the far side of "my pond" in western Massachusetts. Near the east coast of the state, the very same train tracks passed by the world's most famous pond, and when I discovered *Walden* the book, I found I already knew the pond. Thoreau could very well have been describing my pond. I like to think the tracks were a physical link between the two ponds. And Thoreau also coveted his neighbor's land and found a way to both love and possess: "But I retained the landscape, and I have since annually carried off what it yielded with a wheelbarrow." Like all of us he carried a landscape of memories.

Desert Light

O NLY ONCE have I left a water world. I remember well what I thought:

I do not know the desert. I do not know its days and nights, its light and its dark. So I hike along the gravel and sand of a wash and feel both excitement and anxiety. Before me the Saguaro National Park reaches out in dazzling brightness from the foothills of the Tucson Mountains. Behind me in the great bowl surrounded by these mountains, the people of Tucson are busy, as people in any city are busy every day.

I have turned my back on the city and faced the desert. I may think of the people behind me, but none of them are aware of me. Under my feet the gravel crunches. I follow wherever the wash leads. I have no map in mind. On the plane flying in over the Grand Canyon, I studied the flight paths in the airline magazine, and overlaid them with a map of my life travels. They have never taken me this far south, and all have fallen within the temperate zone from New England to the Northwest to old England and Japan. My path has been verdurous; my feet never far from getting wet in puddle, stream, river, lake, or ocean.

But nothing here speaks directly of water in a language that I know, except a dragonfly whose wings reflect the morning sunshine as he helicopters about me. He is a creature who spends the first half of his life as a nymph in water, so I find him an enigma—as I do a butterfly that crosses my path and the crickets that woke me last night from my first desert sleep. They or I are out of sync. It is February, but not the same February I left a day ago when I flew south into the advancing spring.

Here I have no tangled memories, only second-hand images from Tony Hillerman's Navajo mystery novels and the pictures from an aunt's *Arizona Highways* magazines that I retreated to when rain imprisoned me indoors during the long summers of my green years. I find it odd that my one vivid memory triggers an association with rain dripping from leaf-laden trees. What green there is about me is worn only by the cacti: the giant saguaro that seem averse to crowding and the more gregarious prickly pears. They are *Arizona Highways* pictures come alive. Last evening as we drove to the foothills from the airport the setting sun backlit the saguaros on the hilltops where they stood like giants' silhouettes, eerie sentinels awaiting the obsidian desert night whose stars were the brightest I had ever seen. In daylight the saguaro are friendlier and spread about like green Gumbies or stick men caught in a game of freeze tag.

On home ground I am used to walking for hours among slopes of firs followed by even more slopes of firs—a walk that takes me through shifting shadows, where layers of growth progressively filter light that barely touches the fir-needled floor. Here in the desert, I move up and down slopes dotted with saguaro, a land almost without shadow under the morning sun. In the Northwest, ferns, mush-rooms, and mosses grow on and in the corpses of dead firs that rot into new green. Here the staved ribs of dead cacti litter the ground like bones of great beasts, drying to brown dust that sifts among the sand. I miss the green, but I begin to feel the spell of so much light in so much space.

An hour deep into the desert and the sun is noon high, so I turn around and follow the wash back. I am in no hurry, for I've adjusted to the brightness and the breeze that does not whisper through leaves and grass but gently echoes, if you pause, like the sound of the sea heard in a shell. Turned around, the way I came looks different. I could say that, I suppose, about almost every glance back, every retracing and retelling. I realize that in the two hours now of walking, I've allowed the space and its light to etch itself into my past, to mingle now with all those other landscapes. There is often such delight in being touched by the spirit of a new place. I sift a handful of the wash gravel through my fingers, and it sprinkles back to the ground as if untouched.

When I set out this morning, I passed a rock forma-tion on which the ancient Hohokam engraved petroglyphs hundreds of years ago. The early-morning sun cast them in a holy light. I recognized the shapes of animals and men. They spoke from the past, a foreign language whose words escaped me, but the tone seemed clear: they spoke from and for the light of the desert. They are in shadow now as I retrace my steps, but I see them in my mind. In a moment I will rest my legs in the Redemptorist chapel where the words of Hosea are engraved on the wall: "The desert will lead you to your heart where I will speak." I will listen.

Wild Notes

G ATHERING DUST next to worn and often-visited volumes of poetry are a sparrow's nest, a robin's nest, and two cages, neither much larger than a small cup and both made in Japan. The books on the shelf came first; the keepsake treasures found their way haphazardly over many years. And as I look at the books now, I hear faint echoes of nightingales, crickets, robins, grasshoppers, and sparrows: the music of earth made part of poets' music. As I look at the nests and cages, I long for that immediate music of wild notes.

Years ago, I took the sparrow's nest from a birdhouse in our old pear tree. My youngest daughter built the bird-house as a school project, but the sparrow was probably a descendant of a song sparrow we named "Christopher's sparrow," after my son. Through the barely opened bed-room window, the sparrow's sweet, sad, morning song eased my son gently from sleep and dream; something my wife and I could never do. The pensive and dreamy boy found a kindred spirit in the alternately melancholy and joyous song of the bird. My son, now grown, has flown from home, so the saved nest has become a fragile physical link to his childhood. Like the song of the bird, it seems so simple: bits of straw and grass woven into a bowl that can be held in an open palm but not grasped.

I never replaced the birdhouse when it finally rotted away, and I have never found another nest. But the sparrow's progeny still sing when my visiting son sleeps in his old bedroom. At my seasonal chores out-of-doors, a song sparrow often greets me as if time never passes. Neither he nor I tire of his song repeated over and over.

Robins, seasonal neighbors to my sparrow, seem less disciplined, or perhaps they are just more effusive and urban. The sparrow sings from the heart of trees or shrubs; and in all his incarnations "Christopher's sparrow" has been a solitary singer, almost always out of sight. But spring and summer, morning and evening, robins flood my neighbor in an elaborate chorus. Their nest, like their song, is a catchall of stuff, and their nests are rather conspicuous in the crooks of one or more of my trees every year. In their case, the size of the choir in no way diminishes the beauty of the songs, and when the leaves fall and robins fall into silence, the air seems as empty as the trees.

Missing their song always brings to mind the boy I once was, a boy enthralled by a puppet show based on the Hans Christian Andersen tale of the Emperor's Nightingale. In the story, enchanted with a wild nightingale's song, the Chinese emperor has the bird captured and restrained with silken cords. Later he is presented with a mechanical bird in a gilded cage, both made by craftsmen from Japan. The wild bird escapes, only to return, saving the life of the

The Play of Light

emperor. His majesty keeps the artificial bird in his palace but still enjoys visits by the wild nightingale, who lives in his garden.

At the time I would have loved to possess a mechanical bird in a cage or even a robin on silken cords, but I settled for a jar of crickets. I filled the jar with grass and then hunted beneath our porch for my musicians. I placed the jar on my bed stand, just as I had at other times with fireflies. But the effect was overwhelming, and I chose the next night's sleep over chirping. I did not realize it at the time, but Japanese artisans, who fashioned the cage and artificial nightingale in Andersen's story world, built tiny cages for crickets in the real world. I have two. One is very old and intricately crafted of split bamboo. Its bars are thinner than toothpicks, and it has a tiny door that slides up and over like those of circus wagons. It was a present from my wife. The second I purchased in Japan. It is plastic, gaudy green, cheap, and, from my own observations, a necessity for children of a certain age in Japan who fill them not only with crickets but also with cicadas and exotic beetles that emit nearly inaudible squeaks. In fact, I kept a rhinoceros beetle in my cage as company in my hotel room in Tokyo. And I have been tempted by childhood memories to cage a cricket again, but just tempted.

Better yet, there is an old friend of mine who had the good fortune to share a winter with a cricket who found its way into the cellar. Her grandchildren would listen with her on cold nights when only the wind played out of doors. The cricket warmed the house with late summer notes almost until spring. What became of it I do not know, but my friend told her grandchildren that she left the doors open so it could find its way back outside where they could hear its chirp again at the end of the next summer.

––•––

At the end of that summer when I removed the sparrow's nest, I walked out into an evening where the last robins were singing as were the first of the crickets. I walked toward the home of an old teacher, a teacher who was also an old man in the last years of his life. He lived at one end of my block and I at the other. He had been a professor of music, a composer, and, in his youth, a concert performer. Until his eyes and hands finally betrayed him, he played to himself evenings on a baby grand in his sparely furnished living room. If the evening was mild, he left his front door open. I often timed evening walks so that they coincided with his playing.

I sat, then, unannounced in what I called the cheap seats, the front porch stairs. Through the open door the old man floated his serenade into the evening. And when he paused, the evening answered with its own wild notes. My day closed where the two worlds of music met, blended, and drifted together into the new night.

To Catch the Days

L OOKING OUT my window at the world of nature I
think, as I often do, of rain, of water, and all the ways
water has touched me. For me it is the most sacramental of the elements: A priest poured water over my infant
forehead before my eyes had fully opened to the world,
and another priest will sprinkle water on my casket when
my eyes are once again closed to the world. But I am in
no hurry for that final sprinkling, and would rather enjoy
the world between blessings for a while longer. Going into
a church I dip my finger into water and again do so leaving, blessing as I do what took place between holy water.
So too in life, and, I like to think, so too in the cathedral
of nature. But I have to keep my eyes open. For there are
sights and sounds that awaken me to the moment, and I
have come to regard them as omens and talismans. Some
come as surprises, once-only occurrences. Others recur,
but choose their own timing: the honking of geese above
the clouds on a cold night, for instance, or the sight of a
hawk up close.

This past fall a heavy rain drove my neighbors indoors
and leaves from the trees. I looked out one afternoon to

see if the mailman had come and saw instead a fox squirrel burying walnuts in the lawn and in newly raked piles
of leaves. As I watched through the window, a hawk dove
out of the rain in a blurred pass at the oblivious squirrel.

Midday, city street, hard rain: all improbabilities for
such an event. And had the hawk not tried twice more to
snatch the squirrel, I would have doubted my eyes. On
the hawk's third pass, the squirrel took alarm and then
refuge in the nearest tree where it chattered invective and
fluffed its tail in defiance.

He or she (I can never tell with squirrels) escaped,
but I didn't. I would never forget what I had seen. The
sight had its talons in me and held me fast. And I in turn
held that day. It would not—like so many days before or
after—merge, blur, or disappear in the routine and blank
verse that are the measure of so much of a life.

I envy that hawk sometimes, wishing my perceptions
had the eyes and talons to stalk and catch the everyday
world I pass through. And even more than that I would
relish the power to bring back the moments in their original glory. What fun it would be to have the powers of a
sorcerer, to be Merlin with command over the memories
of every moment. That sense of command comes too infre-
quently; too many squirrels escape sight as well as capture.

We banished the sorcerers long ago, but we tolerate
and sometimes revere those at the edge of our society
whose hold on the present is not so much magical as spiritual: artists, poets, and holy people of deep faith. In our
rush through our allotted days, they counsel us to walk,
to smell the flowers. And they often pick a handful and
hold them before us.

My father was an artist and made a living at it commercially. He was not a Sunday painter, and he did not ply his art beyond his work. But he was forever illustrating this or that with a pencil on whatever came to hand: paper bags, the margins of a newspaper, a napkin at table. These quick sketches he would crumble and toss away when he made his point. I envied his ability to catch the world and put it on paper, and for some years hoped the skill might be passed on in our genes.

It struck me then, and still does, that a diary or journal of sketches would be a valuable occupation and possession. I would have settled for the ability to sketch my mother's hands, our front stairs—whatever caught my attention on a given day.

One summer spent visiting relatives, I put together a sketchbook, but I had to limit myself to drawing tree leaves. They were the only things I could get right. So I sketched a leaf and named its tree and the date in a small ringed notepad that I kept in my pocket with a pencil stub.

I kept the sketches a secret and planned to give the notebooks as a present to my father at the end of the summer. Somehow I thought that if I mastered drawing leaves the rest of what I saw would progressively admit to my growing skill. My secret was discovered at a family picnic where I drifted off to sketch while the grownups visited. Among the adults was an elderly emigrant Russian artist who painted murals and decorations in Russian Orthodox churches. He was Grampa Sokolov to everyone, even those like me who related to him very distantly.

As I sketched a leaf, Grampa came up behind me and

caught me at my drawing. He was a small, frail old man but had the strong eye and hand I have come to associate with painters and sculptors. He spoke no English and wore baggy trousers with bulging pockets. From one of them he pulled a small sketchbook and opened it to a sketch of leaves. He smiled, patted me on the shoulder, and left me to my drawing.

Having seen Grampa's sketches, I felt less affection for my own, and though I drew leaves for the rest of the summer, the knack of sketching did not bloom as expected, and I never gave the book to my father. I regret that now, and regret also that I did not have an opportunity to get to know Grampa, who saw more in my leaves than I did. These were misfortunes—one an error of youth, the other of circumstance.

But I did not add a third error by putting away forever the pad of paper and pencil stub. I would come to learn that paper is receptive to words as well as lines. And at infrequent intervals I've had at my shoulder someone who has looked at the world as I'd like to, but with a keener eye and sharper pencil.

The late poet William Stafford was like that, and each time he called on the campus where I teach, I thought of his poem "Uncle Bill Visits." His voice, like the pat of Grampa Sokolov's hand, acknowledged that we were at least distant relatives, if for no other reason than our marriage to the same world.

And like Grampa, Stafford had a keen eye and strong hand. The first time I spent alone with him, we walked to the edge of the bluff that runs along the west boundary of our campus. We looked out over the Willamette River at Mt. Hood. A hawk rose from Mock's Bottom directly in front of us and hovered until the air current carried him aloft. He was so close we could see his eyes.

I like to think that the hawk blinked first as he faced us, but my eye was not as keen as the bird's or the poet's. Only they knew.

That day Stafford sat in what had once been a chapel with a group of students. The students let him look over their shoulders at their poetic sketches, the things they had managed to catch from their days. He spoke, as he often did, of his little poems, of getting up before sunrise every morning to write. He was at his liturgy, alert and ready to catch the day before it had hardly begun. He blessed it early. If he preached at all in the site of the old chapel it was the simple message that the day lay before us all and we ought to be alert to its possibilities and little poems. And in his vocabulary *little* was a weighty word, like *prayer*. In his vision and aesthetic the little poem spoke to anything one encountered in the world, and it often allowed the world to speak back.

That night he read to us, as I suppose he must have to thousands of people in his lifetime. He pulled out loose sheaves of poems, emptied his pockets so we could see what he saw.

These were things that didn't get away, the sights and sounds of countless days. And his wry smile while he spoke reminded me of the old Russian artist. It is in the sketching, not the sketch, that we truly cherish something of each day.

They leave us finally, the poets and artists. Yet the days

remain, and it is our misfortune if we choose not to greet and catch what we can.

———

When I was a boy, catching meant butterflies and insects, though in chasing them I spent enough time in the fields and woods to encounter all sorts of wild things. I put away my net and kill jar a long, long time ago, but when a swallowtail sails among the leaves of my linden tree and over to my neighbor's garden I can feel my pulse rise. It would be fun to give chase. I tend to chase other things now—memories, ideas, and words—but old ways die hard. Remembrances elude or find their way into my net much as long-horned beetles and monarch butterflies did. There were things I set out to catch, and so patrolled a field or meadow, net at the ready and eyes alert, screening out anything that might distract me from my quarry. But other times I swept my net through the grass and weeds of a field, swooshing and crisscrossing like a reaper. With a sturdier net I would troll the bottom of ponds. I never knew what I might catch, and sometimes what I netted, I could not identify. Into my jar went what I wished to label and save; the rest I shook into the wind.

I still chase and sweep through the days of my life, still wish to label and save. Both nature and memory still surprise me, and neither lends itself to brief descriptions. But it is hard not to try to attach a label, to define a moment.

One summer while I was picking string beans in my backyard garden, an angry blue jay distracted me. Over the fence and near the road, he was raising an unusual ruckus, even by blue jay standards. As I've gotten older, picking pole beans and trellised snow peas has become an interesting challenge, for the closer I get to the plants the harder it is to see the beans—green gets lost among the green. The jay's tirade made it all the worse, so I went to the road to see what all the fuss was about.

He was on the grass of the parkway and then hopped below the curb into the gutter, where all I could see was a flurry of wings. When I stepped into the road, he flew into the nearest tree and addressed his hostility to me. Originally it had been directed at a mole that must have emerged from the lawn and tumbled into the gutter where he was stranded, a wall and floor of concrete. His movements were feeble. I returned to the garden for my spade with which I scooped up the now limp mole. I placed him under a bush where I thought he could make his way into the safety of my neighbor's garden bed. But as he rolled off the blade of the spade, I could see a dark gash in his side where the jay had pecked at him. His insides were beginning to spill out; he stopped moving. The jay in the meantime continued to harangue me. Had I picked one less bean, would this little drama have played out differently? Could I have been a *Deus ex machina,* rescuing the disoriented mole and perhaps changing in some small way the natural history of the neighborhood? I leaned on my spade and mused, like the poet Burns who disturbing a mouse's nest two centuries ago asked what to make of "the best-laid schemes o' mice an' men." The temptation is to link, to find the proper analogy or parable, to give the moment meaning.

I did not quite know what to make of the mole and the jay, who usually dwell in such different realms of air

The Play of Light

and earth. Gratuitous violence is not an unusual pattern in either the world of nature or men, but this curbside encounter was extraordinary. Even in the world of moles a wrong turn hazards fatality. As I picked beans on a lovely summer's day, death was all around me; only when I stepped back did I notice it. But the jay interrupted again, one more tirade before he went off to other mischief, for that is the way of jays. And I took the encounter with me and finished my bean picking.

There was another encounter among the same beans. Our kitchen window overlooks the garden, and one evening my wife called my daughter and me to come look. In our home the very phrase "come look" anticipates something special or unusual. A small falcon was perched on the horizontal pole where I had strung the twine for blue lake and red runners. He was absolutely still. And then my daughter pointed and added another "look." Above the head of the hawk a hummingbird circled, perhaps as curious as we were and certainly unconcerned. The hawk ignored him, grew bored perhaps, and finally glided off into the dusk. The hummingbird sipped from the red runner blossoms. We returned to whatever we were doing.

Without the hawk and the hummingbird, I fear that day would have been like one of the beans I picked and dropped into the basket with all the others, harvested and forgotten, green lost among green. The fate of most days. "Come look." It saved a day, lodged it in memory, perhaps three memories, where it rests like a poem or a sketch in a tattered notebook to which any one of us may turn back someday yet to come. And when we do, the three of us

will still be standing together looking out on the world
through the same window of summer.

———·—

I caught one morning another Cooper's hawk diving out
of the fog to snare, almost at my feet, an unlucky starling.
I was close enough to see the fierce glint of his eyes and
perhaps sense his dilemma: to give up the prey and fly,
or to hang on to breakfast and deal with this bifocaled
professor—that was the question. He opted for a series
of short hops among the campus shrubs in an endeavor
to escape *and* eat his breakfast. I followed until he finally
took flight (without the rest of his starling). I had never
been so close to a hawk.

I knew, even as the Cooper's knifed away through the
campus trees, that I would share the episode at my supper
table, and the hawk would find its way into my teaching.
And I knew that I would borrow from Gerard Manley
Hopkins's sonnet "The Windhover":

> I caught this morning morning's minion, king-
> dom of daylight's dauphin, dapple-dawn-drawn Falcon, in
> his riding

Soon I will ask a class to turn to the Hopkins poem on
page 976 of *The Norton Anthology of Poetry* to read his
hawk poem, and to hear about my hawk. Every year I
ask a class or two to study the poem with me. Like most
college teachers, I work within a predictable yearly cycle
of courses and within the courses I regularly revisit certain works, some for pedagogical reasons, some because

they are personal favorites. My calendar is not unlike the liturgical calendar that has its seasons and whose days acknowledge particular saints, martyrs, Church fathers with special readings and prayers from the Old and New Testaments. Most days I turn to one of the heavy volumes from *The Norton Anthology* to read from and about a poet, novelist, or playwright—all the saints, minor and major, of English literature.

In my life the hawks came long before poetry. I had never seen Hopkins's British windhover, but I knew well the sparrow hawk, the American kestrel, having watched them perched on phone wires along country roads. From the back seat of the family's Bel Air, I endured my father's driving by seeking out the sleek sparrow hawks and their hefty cousins the red-tails. I could see the speckles on the breast, the curved talons, and the fierce eyes.

It was a sparrow hawk that came to mind when I sat in a long-ago classroom, spellbound as my Jesuit-trained teacher intoned the fourteen lines of the sickly British Jesuit's poem from memory:

> Of the rolling level underneath him steady air, and striding
> High there, how he rung upon the rein of a wimpling wing
> In his ecstasy! then off, off forth on swing,
>> As a skate's heel sweeps smooth on a bow-bend: the hurl and
>> gliding
> Rebuffed the big wind.

I did not catch all that I could in that first hearing, but I saw the sparrow hawks and the Cooper's of my time and place, remembering again the thrill of those hunters in flight. And then my teacher began the poem again, word by word, and he seemed at the time an adept sculptor who chiseled away all that confused so that what remained was polished and hard as marble. I did not misread the poem, but I believe I misread my teacher. I envisioned passing from teacher to teacher, all carvers, who would show me how to cut to the statue buried in the words. But when I became a teacher and looked for poems as well as hawks, I found reading and teaching were not chiseled but modeled, words built like clay on the armature of the first reading.

I try to share some sense of this with my students as I read on:

> My heart in hiding
> Stirred for a bird,—the achieve of, the mastery of the thing!

Isn't life connected? I ask them. The present carries the past; memory and present experience collide as well as evolve. And then, lest we become too abstract, I move the discussion back to the falcon that moved the hiding heart. I can in this instance direct their gaze from the classroom window to the spot where the Cooper's hawk stirred my imagination and wonder, or I can send them to the bluff where the red-tails ride the currents from the Willamette before diving on their prey in the rail yards and granaries by the river. Or I suggest the other hawks who fly upon the words of the poets Ted Hughes or James Wright or Robinson Jeffers, hoping that they will do both: walk to the bluff and turn open the pages of poetry anthologies.

I would have the world and the word merge as Hopkins does:

> Brute beauty and valour and act, oh, air, pride, plume, here
> Buckle! AND the fire that breaks from thee then, a billion
> Times told lovelier, more dangerous, O my chevalier!

As the hawk dives all the elements connect, buckle together, and Hopkins's exclamation points spring naturally from his awe—a troubled awe that is the wellspring of his poetry. So I sketch the man, the priest torn between a scrupulous and nearly neurotic piety and an almost hedonistic and pantheistic attraction for the wonder of creation. In his vision each flower, bird, and person carries a defining uniqueness, yet all of creation rhymed for him like a great poem. He found it all about him, and conveyed it in the understated and elliptical closing lines of "The Windhover":

> No wonder of it: sheer plod makes plough down sillion
> Shine, and blue-bleak embers, ah my dear,
> Fall, gall themselves, and gash gold-vermilion.

There is no end to the wonder of the world: We see it in the gleam of the plow blade polished and eventually worn away by the friction of cutting through the earth; we see it in gray embers as they fall and momentarily flame; we see it in the fierce swoop of the falcon. Beauty but no prettiness or delicacy. Hopkins penned a dedication between the title and first line: *To Christ our Lord.* There was the birth at Bethlehem; there was also the crucifixion at Golgotha. This was the rhyme Hopkins saw. He caught the world God gave him and gave it back as best he could with words. I like to think my students raise their eyes from the poem more open to the rhymes of words, the world, and its creator, but rather than say this, I recite one last time:

I caught this morning . . .

II

Among the Living and the Dead:
Epiphanies of Time and Memory

Dark Room

I SAT ONCE in a memory chamber. Or so it seemed to me. It was a photography darkroom in an art museum. Darkness was total in the small room, and I did my best to be absolutely quiet while my daughter struggled to wind undeveloped film on a plastic spool, which apparently was defective. She was frustrated and angry. She would not give up, which would mean losing the film, nor would she let me help (stubbornness runs in the family).

In the darkness I thought of how much easier it is sometimes to guide the students that I teach than my own children. I thought of my daughter. All summer long she had been shooting rolls of 35mm film for the photography class that she attended Saturday mornings at the art museum before her stint as a lifeguard, her summer job while she was home from college. When the mood struck her, she developed prints at night in the museum's darkrooms. I usually dropped her off and then picked her up; she hadn't learned to drive a stick shift so she needed my taxi. But that night she let me tag along. It had been a long time since I had kept her company rather than just drive her somewhere. We'd had a year of estrangement, and neither of us knew how to talk about it.

We drove that evening from the inner city pool where she watched over other people's children, kids she'd pulled choking from the deep end, kids who hung around after their swim to walk her to my van when I picked her up. Tonight we had to stop at the fountain by the sports arena so she could finish off her roll of film.

I helped her set up a tripod so she could catch the jets of water exploding from the fountain. And then she took pictures of kids riding bikes through the spray. These are the last pictures on the roll she is now struggling to keep on the spool. The other pictures were of her brother, her mom, and the dogs. They were, she said, her best pictures ever. She hadn't taken my picture. I tried not to think about that.

She kept her developed pictures separate from the albums and the many boxes that house all the pictures I've taken, so many that it was easier to store them in boxes like files. Negatives I store separately. At first the files recorded an orderly chronology of the family, our still life documentary of early marriage, holidays, babies, sports, graduations. The usual I suppose. But over the years the kids have quite naturally disregarded my pleas to keep the photos in order as they shuffled through them on rainy days or pilfered them for their school projects or traveled with them on their own sentimental journeys. (These journeys surprise me. They shouldn't, but they always do.) Admitting defeat, I have given up trying to keep the photos in any kind of order or expecting anyone else to, and now jumbled and reshuffled they have grown more like the family's memory than its history.

And when I've shuffled through the boxes myself, looking for some clue or trigger to the past, I can tell which of my three children has journeyed among the photos most recently: At one end of the box there will be a short stack featuring the searcher. Sitting in that museum darkroom, I didn't even have to close my eyes to conjure one of them sitting on the rug of my study, usually in bathrobe and slippers, a little person bent over a meager past already puzzling out the chapters of a short life.

But maybe I am mistaken and "meager past" is a bad choice of words; the past is a box always full, it's just that the box gets bigger as we get older. I, too, bent over albums in flannel pajamas and Indian moccasin slippers. My parents kept the old imitation leather albums and loose prints in the single drawer of the mahogany veneered coffee table that accompanied them until they were only pictures themselves. My brother has the table now, a thousand miles from where I sit in darkness, and those albums are scattered among the family. Some of the pictures are in my boxes, and my children must encounter my past just as I did my parents'.

It looks as if my daughter will be this generation's photographer. Like my father before me and his father too, she got the bug early. Which means she will begin to disappear from the family photos. Who takes the picture of the picture taker? My father is conspicuously absent in the hundreds of shots of my family. He must be fixed in my children's minds only by those few shots where he managed to coordinate his flash, timer, and mad dash from the tripod back to the posed family. Economically, he bought discounted flash bulbs. What he thought he saved for light, he paid for in film. Invariably he would make his mad dash only to pose us while the camera ticked down to its click, but without the accompanying flash. When we were teenagers we teased and complained so much through these misfires that my father took fewer and fewer pictures.

Only one photo remains of my father's father. Before her death, my mother divided the family photos among the three brothers. My brothers have most of the pictures, but I have all of the negatives, hundreds and hundreds of them in envelopes cut in strips about the length of bookmarkers. I have only a Xerox of the oldest prints sent to me from my middle brother, a page of ghostly images, too stark in their black and white. Grandfather stands on a beach with his arms around his wife and a teenage girl who would become my aunt. Three younger children sit at their feet. I recognize my father and my uncle as the two seated boys. We never thought to ask about the girls or the beach, and there is no one left to tell who they were.

My uncle must have been three or four, so the picture was taken about 1911 or 1912. There he stands: the man my father was named after, and I after my father, and my son after me. He is shorter than his wife Marie, the Eve of our line, who wears what is most likely a bathing suit but resembles a dark bloused dress with short sleeves and a belted waist. And the Adam of our family: a wiry, mustached Frenchman in old-fashioned swimming togs, a T-shirt affair worn outside long trunks that extend mid-thigh. The bony knees could be my father's, my son's, or mine. The smile I have seen on my father and in mirrors.

Grandfather looks so ordinary and happy. Not the man who cooked his wife's pet doves for a family dinner or the man separated from his family before he died or the man who got my seminarian father drunk to torment his estranged wife. But there he is, skinny legs and all, the retired soldier, the legendary cook, the failed businessman, the failed husband. And none of this is obvious in the photo. Only the picture remains and the stories my brothers and I might repeat to our children. Who can be sure of what they will remember? I fear the picture will outlast the stories. But what will the picture become without a story? An old marker; a gravestone read by strangers.

In the artificial night of the darkroom, I pulled out the old stories and pictures, but my daughter slammed the narrow counter in frustration, and the inside of the darkroom trembled with her frustration. She was in tears, I could tell. "I can't do it. I can't do it," she sobbed. A roll of film, thirty-six pictures of her mother, her brother, her dogs, a fountain, a past hardly past, the harvest of her happiness and anxiety: keepsakes, memories, the busy work that distracted her while her mother and father tried to put their lives in order. She held more than film in her hands. I knew what she felt. There are times in our lives when we need to gather tangible records. Perhaps with age we need them less and turn more and more to the album of memory.

I spent a summer when I was much younger than she with my uncle (the boy who sits on the beach next to my father in the old photo) and his wife Ruth. It was a summer spent adding to my collection of butterflies and moths that I planned to enter, as I did every summer's end, in the local museum's nature competition. The night my aunt and uncle brought me home, I spread my boxes of pinned beauties on my bed to show my mother and father. And they were beauties: lunas, underwings, Polyphemus, Cecropia, and even an emperor. I was so proud and felt as accomplished as I ever have. But I had laid the cases over the belt of my bathrobe and as my parents left me to get ready for bed, I lifted the robe and the belt pulled the cases over the edge of the bed. They and the beauties and the happiest summer of my childhood smashed across my bedroom floor. There was nothing really my parents could do; they soothed as best they could by saying little. They knew enough not to lecture about providence, learning lessons. Before I pulled the robe from the bed, I felt I would keep the butterflies and moths forever. I lost them all but kept the memory of that night, that childhood disappointment, more vividly than any other from those years.

And I did not want my daughter to lose her pictures. I would rather a different memory color that summer. I wanted to reach out to her in the dark, hold her as I did when she had night terrors as a child, eyes open but caught in a terrible dream. I would hold the child no longer a baby in my arms and walk and sway till sleep or wakefulness released her, then set her down with gentle words into a gentler dark. But she was too old now and my legs were nearly asleep from holding still.

"Can you roll the film back?" No she couldn't and has already told me so. Can't I remember anything? A harder question than she supposed. I remembered too much: all that has happened between pictures, all the undeveloped rolls of my life. But with the tears over she was open to suggestion, and all I could think of was covering the film somehow while I searched for another spool, hoping that some other student had since returned one to the class's shared locker. So she put the film in the canister without the spool, and I managed to find her backpack beneath the plastic chair. In the dark we zipped the canister in the backpack and the backpack in the plastic bag that lined the wastebasket under the counter. All this we did blind, but together.

We shifted places so that I could open the door. I have vague memories of blind man's bluff as a child or with this child; I'm not sure which. I found the door handle and stepped out quickly from the blackness into the red light of the space that separates the three darkrooms from the door to the main hall. My daughter closed the inner door behind me, and I hurried to the main lab and grabbed three spools, which I handed into the darkroom where my daughter worked now under the glow of a red lamp.

I closed my eyes. I had spent my daughter's life waiting for her, rarely with a camera but always with images of her, even when I couldn't see her. At hospitals, dentists' offices, churches, schools, friends' houses, playgrounds: I had waited at every hour of the day and night. There was a box of these images put away like the patrimony of negatives I've stored in the back of my closet, beneath my overcoats. It is while I waited that I shuffled through that box, and the pictures felt to me like cards my children dealt when we played "Go Fish" so long ago. I was surprised not so much by the cards but by the hand they formed.

I did not wait long. My daughter nudged my shoulder, and whispered, "Dad?" She had saved her film and was already halfway down the hall to the photo lab to print them by the time I stood. I trailed behind watching the happy bounce of her backpack and waited to see what would develop. But I wondered what would become of her pictures of her memories. Someday I will be but a picture in an album (or in a computer file), or a character in one of my children's stories, or a memory, just like my father and mother before me. And I think of them.

Among the Living and the Dead

M ANY YEARS AGO and before my mother died, I
spent a summer in Tokyo. August that year was
unusually hot and rainy, a season of uncomfortable days.
But the evenings were clear, and I celebrated as an outsider
the Oban festivals, All Souls festivals, both in the city and
in the countryside. I must have sent my mother post cards
and certainly a birthday card, but I have no specific memory of thinking about her during my stay in Japan.

I have yet to return to Tokyo, but during August I
attended an Oban festival in the local Japanese Garden
where a Buddhist monk chants before an altar placed on
an ached bridge. Sometimes a Catholic priest stands silently by his side. Water flows under the bridge from a
pond. A bell punctuates the monk's prayers. This year I
attended on August 8. August 8, 1910 was my mother's
birth date. She died in 1992, seven years after my father.
I thought especially of my mother. I thought: Now I too
move among the living and the dead.

It took me a very long time to articulate that thought,
which had for much of my life fluttered in the shadows
of my consciousness like the moths drawn to the pond by

The Play of Light

the oncoming darkness and the candles that illuminated the monk's sutras. Other kindred thoughts drifted from the darkness as if also drawn by altar candles. There were old thoughts, very old memories, but on this night gentle ones. I remembered also a line the poet Dylan Thomas wrote about his own childhood innocence: "Time held me green and dying / Though I sang in my chains like the sea." Mercifully time shelters most of us from a sense of our own death, some more than others. My innocence was prolonged; I took longer to piece the puzzles of life and death together. But the pieces were always spread before me.

A very early memory: My father leaves us to travel to his mother's funeral. I have no image of that last living grandparent other than photographs; the other three had died long before my mother or father even met. It is a very vague memory, an inexplicable troubling that I have always been able to recall. After that my experiences with the dead were mostly sacramental and unusually numerous.

Ours was a traditional Catholic family and our home was across the street from the parish church. As soon as I made my first communion, I was enlisted in the ranks of altar boys. And because I lived so close to church, I was drafted to do more than my share of morning Masses. Though this was never stated, as I grew older, the priests had me serve at an unusual number of weddings and funerals as compensation, I believe, for all those early mornings. The weddings meant a tip; the funerals a morning off from school.

I did quite well, if one measured by tips; my photos of the time show a boy surprisingly angelic (an irony not lost to my mother). Looking back I know the real irony was that I was almost a weekly witness to the mysteries that would and still do perplex me: love and death. At the Masses that were then always part of the wedding and funeral liturgies, I rang the bell, not knowing the haunting reality of tolling my own destiny.

There were times, late in my altar boy days, when I felt, or thought I felt, a calling to the priesthood, and I seriously reflected on the meaning of the rituals. But those were late and rare, and I believe that like most altar boys, I reacted much like a professional actor in a long-running and serious drama. I had my lines of Latin to master and the intricate choreography of the Mass, service for the dead, and the burial itself. I never knew the dead person, so I focused on the living mourners and the priest who expected me to be as inconspicuous and dignified as possible and to have the censer and holy water within easy reach. Only liturgically was I an insider.

Death itself became real when my first pet, a stray kitten that my mother really didn't want me to keep, was torn to pieces by a pack of neighborhood dogs. I found its body in a neighbor's yard and cried my heart out in anguished and unanswered prayers (the first of many times in my life). The first human corpse I saw was the pastor of the parish where I went to school. The nuns shepherded all eight grades of the school through the back door of the rectory into the kitchen, down a hall, into the front sitting room where we knelt on a prie-dieu, and then out another hall and back through the kitchen. It was not particularly distressing, just strange, and I remember more of the kitchen and its utensils than the viewing room with its heavy odor of flowers, the rouged face, and the cotton in the old priest's nostrils.

The realization that I could die came later. The father of one of my school friends was an undertaker. Sometimes we would walk after school the short distance to the family funeral home to hitch a ride home in one of the limos or even in the back of the hearse where we would spin the rollers as if they were the dials of a plane and we were bombardiers. But one day my friend took me to his father's office by way of the preparatory room with its steel table and apparatus. Nightmares and much comforting by my parents followed. I would, of course, eventually sleep peacefully, but I had felt the certainty of my mortality for the first time, and night, sleep, and death then became forever intertwined.

In high school about the time I left service as an altar boy, I began to read seriously and to run on the cross-country and track teams. I lived in a city, and the closest off-street practice courses were the park or the cemetery; I usually chose the cemetery, especially in the early morning and evening. Alone and undisturbed I ran the narrow tree-lined lanes that looped in and out almost like a maze. Often I did not know quite where I was among the grave markers that crowded the greens; in trying to reestablish my bearings by sighting a familiar tree or mausoleum, I registered the numerical implications of so many grave markers, dating back and further back. Alive, these people could and did populate a small city. I would slow my pace sometimes and repeat random names and dates, wondering as I did if I might be the only one in the world who had spoken the name in decades and wondering also what that might mean.

I wandered also in those days among the stacks of the public library, which then and now emit to me a musty scent of a past accumulated in the books whose pages have been touched and turned by as many fingers as old dollar bills. Sometimes more greedily, at least in my case. I read Tolkien and Stevenson. Then Dickens and Faulkner and Updike. I traveled imaginatively among characters that lived long before my time in books written by authors already dead. In reading, the past was present. As long as the book lived, the author somehow seemed alive.

There is an awesome illusion in the eternal present of a book, and I envy those who have left behind pages as well as a name and dates carved in stone. How few people are fortunate enough to leave behind a book, and yet how many books there are. In a lifetime one could no more read the names of all the books written than the names of all the people who have ever lived. The immense populations of the living and the dead grow apace. In literature they merge.

I found mirrors in literature; among poems and stories, a reflection of myself often startled me. John Updike's "Pigeon Feathers" threw my own adolescent face and fears back at me. I read his story of a fifteen-year-old Lutheran boy, David, who cannot find an adult who will give him a comforting answer about the dead, God, and God's concern for him. The best his parents and minister offer him is that we live on in others' memories. Apparently his Lutheran pastors, much like the Catholic ones of my youth, could be descriptive about the afterlife of the damned but remained rather vague about the afterlife of the saved. David wants signs, and finds them and his solution to the mystery of God and death in the intricacy and beauty of the world—in the apparent care the Creator bestowed in a single pigeon feather.

Having spent a life teaching literature, I confess, like David, to the seduction of beauty and intricacy, but have found it illusory at the graveside. As I grow older, it is not beauty but rather memory that comforts me, even as it pains me.

Standing across from the priest at the lip of my parents' graves, I heard the words: "To shine on those who sit in darkness and the shadow of death, to guide our feet into the way of peace." Though I had attended many funerals, until my father's death I do not think I had stood with mourners in a cemetery since my altar boy days. Ironically I had visited more tombs and graves in British cathedrals and Japanese cemeteries. The passage from altar boy to tourist to mourner struck me as odd. And grief itself became for me a jumble of odd thoughts. With the priest's final "Amen," I was left with nothing but memories. At fifteen I could not imagine the power of memory. Among the odd thoughts that I had at the graveside was, Would someone remember me as intensely as I then remembered my parents? And if I were remembered, that might not be the equivalent of heaven, but it would be an enviable fate.

At fifteen and a rather ordinary adolescent, I thought of myself usually in the present or the future. Four times that age I typically tend to look backwards. Younger, I associated dying with night and sleep; older, I associate the dead with words and memory. There is the whole of literature, but there are other words engraved all around us. The campus where I teach is literally a product of inscribed memory. Each morning I walk among buildings that bear names. I note one: Waldschmidt Hall. For my students and most of the faculty, Waldschmidt Hall is where administration and university paperwork takes place. But for me it revives the vivid memory of Bishop Waldschmidt himself, who was president when I first came to the university. His roaring laugh, the sly wink behind the shine of his glasses, the heavy arm on my shoulder: all flash back in a name.

"In memory of": Statues, offices, classrooms, water fountains, plaques, and shrines across the campus bear the inscription. In time, other objects bearing the "gift of" or simply by being engraved trophies or dated group photographs become "in memory of." And when you have spent a good part of your life in a place, you see it as a series of superimposed pictures, peopled in ways that are unseen by newcomers. Communal events with their inevitable reminiscence link us to the dead. This spring an old teaching friend came to tears in the middle of his retirement speech when he remembered a colleague who died when many of us were younger. And for a moment while my friend regained his composure, the dead colleague flickered in the minds of all of us who knew him. How often we wake the dead, or the dead awake in us.

I am a creature of strict habits, and Sundays I tend to sit in the left side aisle of my church, under a window. Often the sun shines through and washes my hand and missal with muted colors from the stained glass, in which St. Ann bends over her young daughter Mary. On the wall next to the window, Jesus meets his mother in the Fourth Station of the Cross. The church is one of the oldest in

Portland but not very old or large if measured by Old World standards. I've walked the side aisles of those medieval cathedrals, amazed at the profusion of crypts and graves. When I toured, there were considerably more dead bodies than live in those ancient churches. Not so in my church, where the most conspicuous memorials are the small brass plates on the prayer rest of the pews. Each Sunday I read *IN MEMORY OF ANTE AND EVA J___*, followed by what must be the names of their children: *Milan, Mary, John, Lesandra, Vincent.* By now those children are also dead.

After the bells of the consecration and an offering to God the Father, the liturgy of the Mass includes a remembrance of the faithfully departed. In my old missal the prayer reads: "Remember also, O Lord, your servants N. and N., who have gone before with the sign of faith, and rest in the sleep of peace." In the missal the Ns are printed large in red. As a boy standing in a pew between my parents, I would pray for the anonymous Ns, unaware of the long list of names that my parents must have remembered. I have a long and growing list now, beginning with my parents and sometimes including the family of Ante and Eva, who have become my surrogates for all who have gone before me.

I have come late in life to where I believe my mother arrived very early in hers. She lost much of her family as a youngster and carried with her both a sense and a memory of the dead. Perhaps because she lived so long among the dead, she joined them peacefully. As I make my way, as we all must, toward her, I think of her as moving not into the future but back into her past, into her memories, and leaving me ahead.

This thought I carry with me as I also carry a lighted candle to the pond in the Japanese Garden on the night of the Festival for the Dead. The monk chants under a clear sky and a bell rings. In procession I walk in darkness to the edge of the pond where I launch the candle and Styrofoam holder and stand in silence with the living. My candle floats out with the other candles, all bright spots on the black water among the reflections of summer stars.

On a Sunday Afternoon

REMEMBRANCE COMES and goes like the stars, eclipsed sometimes by the glow of the present but returning as surely as a night sky. Though we seem to stay put, the night sky above has its seasonal constellations. So too does a mind have its seasonal remembrances.

Especially for me, Sundays in fall. One October, I sat with my married daughter in the top row of general admission bleachers watching the university's women soccer team play a Sunday-afternoon game. A day gray and rainy, but a game close enough to dispel the annoyance of the intermittent drizzle. A scoreless game. The possibility of overtime. But before that there were the innumerable pauses—the almost-ritual throwing the ball back into play after it was kicked out of bounds, the setting-up of players for penalty kicks—pauses where my mind wandered off to play other games.

I replayed another Sunday afternoon many years ago, when this daughter by my side was not yet in school, though there was then, in her bearing and carriage at four years old, a prophecy of the science teacher she would become. On that summer afternoon, perhaps just before the sumptuous dinner her mother would spread before us, we walked around the block, hand in hand, and chatted in that discourse of questions and observations that awkwardly but affectionately bridges the years and mismatched perceptions of child and adult.

We walked in the neighborhood only a few blocks from where the soccer stadium would be built and where my daughter would attend college. But her college years were a long way off then. We made our way round the block; took note of the neighbors' flowers; waved to the retirees who perhaps saw their grandchild in my child; and sought out the midpoint of our promenade—a very little house raised above the sidewalk on a slope where an old couple (was it Cliff and Mabel?) lived with their dustmop of a dog (Shaggy?). And we would visit together, I with Cliff and my daughter with Shaggy, and then turn the corner for home, neither of us keeping the score of our simple happiness or hearing the ticking of the timekeeper's clock.

But the game goes on eternally, and another pause in the action allowed me to walk hand in hand with my father after a morning Mass into the first bright hours of a Sunday afternoon, on our way to my parents' first house, a white house on a hill just beyond the small town where first my mother and then her children would grow up. And my father would walk me from the country church to a bridge over the Housatonic where we would throw sticks, like Christopher Robin and Winnie the Pooh watching to see whose raced out of sight first. Or later when we moved into town, we would walk from church over a bridge on the same river to the main street and the hotel drugstore, where my father would buy each week one Cuban cigar, one *New York Times,* and one Hershey bar, which I was to finish by the time we walked home lest my mother worry that it would spoil my appetite for Sunday dinner. And just to make sure I finished the Hershey bar, we would stop to watch trains in the rail yard at their work; unlike us, they did not observe the Sabbath. All afternoon my father would page though his paper, the Havana smoke drifting from his easy chair, intimating autumn and burning leaves, so that now the odors of cigars and leaf-fires and all the memories they evoke are folded over in me like the multiple, thick sections of my father's *Times.*

My father told stories of his immigrant father, our family patriarch from Marseilles, who had soldiered in the Far East as a young man and who would take the boy who was my father to stretches of sand along the shore of Atlantic City where they first lived. Grampa would smoke a cigar on the way and carried either a small-bore shotgun or a bugle, the one keepsake from his army years. The shotgun meant my namesake grandfather intended a little harmless poaching, a duck or two added to the week's larder if the opportunity presented itself. The bugle meant the playing of the French charge and taps and reveille, tunes he would eventually teach my father to play. When my father told the tale, I could see him in his boy's short pants charging down a sand dune with a curved piece of driftwood for a saber. But that was long, long ago, and there are no more charges for him.

Then there was the final whistle in overtime and the wrong team charged across the field in victory. My daughter and I watched our team leave the field in the slow pace of honorable defeat. We were tired too, spent from the excitement of the game, and saddened by the outcome. As we drove through the campus in the gathering darkness, the afternoon had become a memory and the gym and student union appeared empty. In the windows of the library, students bent over their books and into the coming weeks. The final whistle had blown for the weekend's free time, too.

I drove home along the Willamette River, into the night, hoping my daughter might join us for supper. The nearly deserted campus was behind us, and over the river I noticed ducks, safe now from the old French poacher, winging their way into the dark.

Letters from the Past

THERE ARE TIMES when remembrance catches me
not as a returning constellation but as an unexpected
shooting star. The past has ways of sneaking up and sur-
prising me. In part because I have come to think of myself
as a man of letters—old-fashioned letters—and my em-
brace of the computer has been reluctant and argumenta-
tive. Among my peers, old dogs who have learned new
tricks more readily than I, refrains about the efficiency
and speed and convenience of e-mail have nearly won me
over. Yet I lament the loss of the tactile; the very envelopes,
stamps, and sheets of stationery that I find so personal. To
prove my point, I sent a handwritten letter to one of my
more adamant peers, and to my surprise and joy he sent
me a letter from the coast a week later also penned in ink.
I placed the letter in the book nearest to hand.

Today I cannot remember which book. A more cleri-
cal or fastidious mind could easily devise a better system
for storing letters. In fact if asked if I had a collection of
letters, notes, and cards, I would probably answer no,
remembering only a thin file in an office drawer and
an old shoe box in the back of my closet where I've put

away a few very special or official papers and letters. The rather disorganized truth is that I have stored letters and notes for many, many years with the same diligence, haphazardness, and forgetfulness of an autumn squirrel burying nuts. And like the squirrel, I retrieve my treasures sometimes more by accident than design. I suppose early on I felt a reluctance to throw away the handwritten words of a loved one, and since there always seemed to be a book within reach, I slipped those handmade words in among book-leaves.

Books are both the tools of my trade and my usual workplace, so I have accumulated, as has every other literature professor I've ever known, an impressive (if worn and dog-eared) library: shelves and shelves of books and among their pages years of accumulated letters and notes placed there from habit or as bookmarks. The cycles of my teaching lead me back to books that have waited patiently for me, sometimes for a decade or more. And as I read the books again, I discover or rediscover those old letters and notes. Many of those discoveries have intertwined in my memory the book and the letter it holds in safekeeping.

The pages of some of the books are brown at the edges, and the sequestered notes and letters have begun to leave a ghostly outline on the pages where they live. I come across notes with drawings "FoR dADdy" sketched and crayoned earnestly by my children years ago. I find in the anatomical eccentricities and anomalies of their stick figures the uninhibited play and confidence of those who sang songs of innocence. Regrettably, as my artists grew more sophisticated, fewer original pictures found their way to my books, but the flowery store-bought cards that replaced them grew from "FoR dADdy" to longer heartfelt messages of young people who penned from experience, often gracefully. Certain favorite books hold more than one drawing of flowers wearing Blake-ean grins or flowered Hallmarks, and it is easy to think of these books as plant presses where special blossoms and nosegays might be preserved between absorbent layers of paper, perfect containers for delicate keepsakes and tangible reminders of the past.

A reread letter like a reread poem or essay layers with each encounter, evoking, finally, multiple or even conflicting responses: nostalgia, joy, sorrow for what might have been or what should be. Some of the letters I have kept carry their own stories. Among these storytelling letters is one from a former student of mine.

She was, as my parents would have said, "a big-boned" young woman and "full of it." Her "wild oats" prompted her one spring to drive her off-road vehicle over and around the university lawns before hitting the road for home and the summer vacation. She had the distinction of being one of the few students I had to fail and who then sincerely thanked me for the failure; she took full responsibility for her irresponsibility, a gesture that made me feel guilty as hell.

At the end of her junior year, she began a losing struggle with cancer, and she died before the Christmas of what should have been her senior year. We had exchanged joshing letters, and her death, like that of a handful of other students I have lost this way, stung with irony and injustice.

Deep in winter two months later I received a short letter from her parents and with it an unstamped envelope addressed to me. She had not been able to mail her Christmas greetings and put them aside where her parents found them afterwards. And so I unsealed the envelope and held the card she had held and let her speak one last time before burying the note in a book.

My father was not much given to letter writing, but he always jotted a note when he gave a gift. We shared a passion for sculpture, something we could argue over relentlessly as other fathers and sons might over baseball. I have half a shelf of books about Rodin that my father picked up in used bookstores and presented as special presents. And I've left in some the accompanying card. More than a picture, his handwriting brings him back to me. He closes always with "Love, Dad." And, of course, I do. The "L" of "Love" is hooked at the top in a script of his own devising, an "L" repeated every time he wrote the "Louis" of his and my first name, an "L" I imitated for several years in an attempt to be like him.

I have also the long letters of my mother written in her last year when she was given the grace "to put things in order," me among them. Her letters are scattered in my keeping, and I suspect sometimes that I am not quite the guileless squirrel I pretend to be. Had I kept all my old letters together, I fear they might have been too painful to read. Time tripping is a delicate journey not to be taken carelessly, and spread among my books the past surprises me in small doses.

Not long ago I received a letter from the town on the East Coast where I grew up. It was from an old priest, a contemporary of my mother and a family friend, a mentor of my high school days. In the leisure reading rack of the retirement home where he now lives, he happened upon an old issue of a magazine in which I had written a reflection that mentioned my mother's death. Out of the past he sent his condolences and prayers.

As I hold the stiff half-sheet stationery that he always favored, as I read his tight scrawl, I theorize that much of what passes for creative writing might actually be letters to the past—essays to save what has been and to speak to it. If such is the case, they are open letters, shared but unanswerable. But once, in a priestly scrawl, I found the past speaking back to me.

A Gallery of the Heart

I N THE HALLS of public buildings, filled, as they often are, with old paintings and photographs, I find myself looking into the eyes of the past. When I walk the corridors of the administration building at the university where I teach, several presidents of the university stare or smile at me from their official portraits. I knew three of these men in life, the others only by these oil paintings. From time to time, I've imagined personalities and lives from these pictures. And I've done the opposite too: I have created an imagined gallery of portraits of people I've known.

Memory is such a vast gallery of rooms and halls, and in one of the longer halls I hang the portraits of the teachers who taught me. Depending on my mood, a walk down that hall is a nostalgic journey or a running of the gauntlet. My subjects are dead, aged, or far away, but my portraits of them remain highlighted by expressions and intimations of character that I have sketched and colored from my memories. I look at many of these men with affection; at most with a sense of debt and gratitude; at a few with disappointment.

As I grow older, my consideration of those teachers mellows like the varnish on old oils. Some bring a smile, for they were originally sketched in broad caricatures. When I was first a student, long before the days of student evaluations and tenure review, teachers walked on a higher ground that generously allowed for eccentricities in personality and pedagogy that are rare today.

I suppose the first portrait that I hung was of a Jesuit whose long wispy hair and habit of letting his glasses ride near the end of his nose made him appear much older than his middle years. In our eyes, his fussiness, sonorous voice, and nearly spastic gesticulations confirmed our impression of the old. A charitable description of his teaching method might be "associative": His courses had no syllabi, and the textbook provided the sole anchor to impede but not overcome his inclination to drift into whatever struck his fancy on a given day. These might be the history of watermarks, brickmaking in the Middle Ages, London sewers, or the true identity of Jack the Ripper. Papers turned in might or might not be returned, and his approach to grading was a mystery. Nonetheless I keep his portrait for the stories he read. And he read to us often, not because it was easier than lecturing, but because he possessed a rare gift: His voice could lift words from a page and give them life. The voice that droned on during his digressions metamorphosed into the voices of characters in stories. He even created voices for the authors of the essays that he favored. Forty years later, as I turn the pages of Charles Lamb or E. B. White, I hear his voice. The dialects of Faulkner's Mississippians, the brogues of Joyce's Dubliners, and the accent of Dickens's Cockneys were all in his toolbox.

The Play of Light

I would have better teachers, but none that revealed to me as well as he did the resources and potential of the human voice, the infinite complexity and beauty of sound becoming words and words becoming sounds. And this gift and epiphany always bring to mind the image of the professor's almost Dickensian physiognomy.

Like anyone who has attended school over many years, I spent hours attentive to what my teachers said and how they said it, but also to the expressions that played across their faces, the sharing or withholding of themselves in gestures and mannerisms. I suppose I have borrowed or acquired such things from them just as I have from my parents. But some gestures are inimitable and unique. They are reminders, to me at least, that the best teachers are people who share and project through voices and bodies; people who savor the physicality of teaching. Like it or not, teachers become a part of what they teach, and a classroom, at every level, is a studio for the study of faces and figures rather than still lives.

Perhaps recognition of my own middle age and the many years I have already spent in the classroom draw my eyes most attentively to the older men who taught me. I had my share of brilliant young teachers whose eyes glowed with enthusiasm, men confident and at ease with the newest modes of thought, but they were not much older than I was and they listened to the same music, cut their hair as I might, greeted me coming from and going to the gym. Their strengths and weaknesses were my own, magnified only by their newly won degrees and responsibilities. But the older professors wore faces lined in ways as interesting as the texts we scrutinized together. These were men who had endured, men weathered and honed by life and their work.

And before this long line of men, I can call to mind an even longer line of women, nuns, who guided me from the haven of mother and home to the larger world. In grammar school, they were Sisters of the Holy Ghost, and they bent over me in starched and flowing habits that fluttered about my childhood, white like the wings of doves. Sister Elizabeth, Sister Mary Joseph, Sister Theresa, and Sister Margaret: all long dead now. I have no photographs. In the one saved photo of our eighth-grade class, the priest of the parish is seated in a chair and we stand behind him on the church's front steps. Sister stood by the photographer, making sure we all had proper expressions. They were always in the background, but they are in my gallery of portraits. They taught me to read, to count, to write, and to pray—and much else that I have taken for granted. My hand that now presses the letters on a keyboard was first taken through the alphabet, letter by letter, in the hand of Sister Theresa, whom I looked up to and found beautiful, second only to my mother.

Years later when I acquired the height of a man in my still gangly boy's body, I would look down on Sister Susan, who first taught me Shakespeare and who saw the teacher in me years before I would. She would cock her head to look me in the eye, and when she did, I would catch a reflection of a grinning callow boy. She saw something else, as she did with my classmates also. She saw the good men and women that she prayed we could become. When we disappointed those hopes, it was all our doing. Had she and the others in that gallery of devoted women lived longer, I suspect they would have simply prayed longer and harder for us all.

At the end of my gallery, a portrait of one of my last teachers, a man in whose portrait I always see a haze of tobacco smoke. A heavy, broad-shouldered man, he was slightly stooped by arthritis; his glasses were thick and his eyes and hands unsure. A smoker's cough punctuated his monotonous lectures, and it was not unusual for him in the middle of relighting a cigarette to ignite the filter end by mistake. The sudden flame and acrid odor this produced never alarmed him; he would extinguish the filter in the dregs of coffee left in his mug, twist off the soggy filter, and relight the frayed but serviceable stub.

His monotone could not obscure his reverence for the literature that he brought to us. His love for literature manifested itself in the sheer number of books he brought to class, in the way he lifted each book gently from the pile as he recited its lines from memory, and in the way he patted books when he put them down. Each time he did this, he touched many of us as well as the worn covers.

He had a habit of regarding us over his books with kind but mournful eyes that apparently saw more through thick lenses and hazy smoke than we could imagine. Like the nuns who first taught me, I think he could see what we had been before and what we might become (and not all of it blessed). He read our faces while we read his, all of us stories.

Through the smoke and mounting years, that old professor still regards me with mournful eyes. He has one more lesson to teach me: We all touch others' lives, and each life is a vast gallery of memory. And in those galleries, what will be revealed, what will be remembered about us?

Back in the Day

N OW, SOMEWHAT SURPRISED, I find myself peering through glasses observing and listening to
young people, my son and daughters, other people's sons
and daughters. "Back in the day," my children josh as they
dredge up some gross or glorious memory from grammar
or high school. I also hear the phrase among the college
students I teach, and they inflect it with the same hint
of parody and cool. I quit trying to speak the argot and
patois of the young pretty much after I grew out of their
country, but because I spend time among them, I at least
like to know what their language intends.

A story by Toni Cade Bambara in the early 1970s—
"The Lesson"—is my first recollection of the phrase "back
in the day." Bambara's adolescent narrator reflects on the
bittersweet experiences of growing up in what we now call
an "inner city," and the narrator's "tude" gives her both a
distance and a purchase on the past. My mostly middle-
class students, on the other hand, have probably borrowed
both the phrase and the "tude," like so many other things,
from "the hood."

But their self-deprecation and casualness belie, I believe,

the importance and emotion they attach to memory. They are not so different from old fogies like me as they wish to be. The emotion recollected in humor can mask the spell of the past at odds with their wonderful sense of the present. So "back in the day" is their "once upon my time" and a hedge against sentimentality and a guard against appearing like self-absorbed middle-aged raconteurs. It is a rather low hedge, for we all live in an age eager to leap into nostalgia and sentimentality. They have learned early, if unconsciously, that memories and the past are always tricky stuff, especially tricky to talk about.

———

When my students and I read works of remembrance and nostalgia, works like John Updike's "Pigeon Feathers" and Jamaica Kincaid's "Girl," I ask them two questions that I cannot answer myself: What is your earliest memory? Can you remember the first time you were aware of remembering? While my students are a few decades closer to these childhood events, their memories, like mine, don't permit easy thumbing-back or scrolling, and the book may fall open on an unexpected page, as mine does.

I also ask them if they keep a diary or journal. To those who confess the practice, I ask if they have ever had a run of detailed entries interrupted for several days and then tried to go back and recreate those days. So often, one discovers, those missing days are wholly lost. There is a retrievable routine, yes—sleep, meals, work, television, travel—but unless something unusual happened, Tuesdays merge, as do weeks, months, years as our past grows.

Periodically I've kept a diary and also a journal in which

I've chosen to save from each day just one detail, image, and scene—something very particular that caught one of my senses. Reading back reveals patterns of my sensing: lots of isolated people observed as I passed them by, the sounds of my children (the favorite background music of my life), and light playing off water or creating a shadow, and anonymous faces in news photographs. Things that might catch and hold anyone for an instant. Reading back also reveals how much I cannot retrieve on demand. On a Tuesday years ago I noted my youngest daughter singing herself to sleep. But what of the rest of that day? I registered thousands of impressions, entertained thousands of associations, but I didn't record them and can never play them back. So a whole section of my daughter's life, a period of my own, is condensed into a single poignant memory.

I've passed through my days as if walking across a meadow picking wildflowers as I go: I've kept the blossoms that caught my eye, but I've also carried away burrs and seeds that attach themselves unnoticed to the my trouser-cuffs or sock-tops. So there are memories I have chosen to save, and others that have, it would appear, chosen me—memories I didn't choose to notice, but that I cannot forget.

How soon nascent memory becomes a cache, a burden, a solace, or a loss. Perhaps a sense of lost memories, and with them chunks of a life, mark the boundaries among the countries of the young, middle-aged, and elderly. Certainly my children and my students have not crossed the boundary of youth, not yet. They are so eager to gobble the present to get to the future, to have a past

The Play of Light

that defines them in some way. They want the varsity letter-jacket, the diploma, the reputation, so that others will remember them. It is the inevitable task of a lifetime: to enjoy and fashion an autobiography and a biography simultaneously.

At certain interludes we gather to share and create through ceremonies that reveal the weight of memory. As spring merged with summer, I sat in the university's wooden chapel as my campus community, not unlike the citizens of a small town, were paying respect to a young man taken from us out of season. The Catholic liturgy, the words of the man's brother and sister, the eulogies offered by his fellow teachers and the university's priest-president—these words composed a shared remembrance. Around a bronze urn that held his ashes, we moved back and forth from our present to his past. Much of what was articulated and felt that day were flowers for all to see and remember; but there must have been unseen burrs and seeds that will later catch us unaware in private elegies long after this communal ode.

Wise Men

I N OUR LIFE among the living and the dead, perhaps the days just after a loss are most difficult to bear. It is time to question whether chance or providence brings lives together. One of my father's cherished beliefs was that special people would appear in our lives when we were in need. Now that I have been a father myself, I guess he shared this belief when I struggled with troubles beyond his help or understanding.

Unremarkably a share of trouble and need has come my way, some of my own making, and so too have special people, bearing gifts. When I was young, I did not think of my father's words as they came true, but I often do now, repeating them, perhaps more in hope than faith, to my own son. In the last three years, death has taken three men who were answers to a father's prayers. They visit my thoughts, often unexpectedly.

Father Casey descends the stairs from his study, booming snatches from *My Fair Lady* as if the old rectory were a stage set and he—tall, gaunt, elegant—were Rex Harrison. He has Professor Higgins's cardigan, his cackling laugh, and his pliable voice, face, and limbs that he arranges to whatever the scene or audience needs. He is a shameless ham. And he is there for me, again and again. Death would come to him as a very old man, one who had been chronically ill and ordained early, for his first bishop feared the worst for his deacon. Some bishops later, Father Casey bent his head to our fears and problems, his long fingers for once still and folded as if in prayer. No matter the problem, he would bend to charity without breaking the spirit of obedience. Always slightly ahead of the thaw that was just beginning to warm the church of our time, he guided with a sense of the world people really lived in and a deeply grasped and scholarly appreciation of Catholicism. I thought of him as *my* Father Casey, but so did hundreds of other troubled souls. At his death he would be honored as a priest's priest—one those whom other Fathers sought out just as we teenagers did. With love and intelligence, he found the words to help others find the simple—but ever painful—truths that might free them from what seemed overwhelming. He gave us the right words and a blessing by his long elegant fingers as he bowed his head to his Father.

Victor carries his three-year-old granddaughter on his shoulder, and she pulls grapes from the trellis over her head. *Uva, Maria.* And she fills her mouth with a sweet grape. *Uva,* she answers, *uva.* I hear them from an upstairs window in the rooms where I lived for a short time above Victor and his wife Bruna. Victor laughs, and it is the laughter of an old but big man who was strong enough to support his family with hard labor when they left northern Italy decades ago. His deep voice touches and eases my own sadness and depression.

Long after I met Victor, I learned that the young men

of his village had been taken to Germany as forced laborers as a punishment for not accepting Fascism. Victor survived the deepest darkness of our time and emerged a quiet man of deep and uncomplicated faith. He would speak of the Germans who were kind to him. He took the world as he found it, looking for and sharing the simple joy of family life, which he extended to anyone who entered his home. Few who sat with him could claim his faith in God or humanity, but few who sat with him could leave his table untouched by his faith.

In awkward English he told stories over Bruna's bread and his home-brewed grappa that burned like his words and shared silences all the way down. He was a man to sit quietly with. At night I sometimes heard Victor and Bruna saying the rosary for all of us. I did not have their faith, but I had no doubt that the small beads in Victor's callused hands made the world more humane. I could believe that we are all blessed by the lives and prayers of a good man.

Fred watches me over our lunch in the Museum Restaurant, though for him lunch is not quite the right word. Everywhere we have eaten, the waitresses have convinced the cooks to prepare something off the menu, a soft meal, a small meal that somehow keeps Fred alive. When we leave, both cook and waitress will probably see us to the door and give Fred a hug (this after a bowl of soup or a cup of custard). And Fred knows their stories, like he knows my son's and mine. He is not a priest and has never had a family.

And once again he listens and laughs and encourages.

At Fred's eightieth birthday, hundreds gathered to celebrate—professors he had taught with, waitresses, his mechanic, doctors, lawyers, young people and old: all people whom Fred had helped along their way. My guess is that Fred's early days were rather like young St. Augustine's. He grew up alternately practicing the religions of his parents: mother Catholic, father Jewish. I suspect he left both faiths behind when he went to college. He was not a religious man. Fred was not laying away good works toward heaven; he didn't believe in it. Yet he was spiritual and believed in people and in art. He was cranky, grumpy, sardonic, cynical, and lovable. He listened, he helped—an old teacher who retired from the classroom to the world at large. He was the one man who arrived at a time when both my son and I needed him. He died on the day before Christmas, an anniversary that will be impossible to forget.

I mourn him and mourn my son's loss, which is so much greater than my own. Fred took the place of a grandfather for my son, helping my son through his teens in ways that I never could. And now my son is just beginning to live among the dead as well as the living. I can only repeat for both of us my father's belief that special people will appear in our lives when we need them. We both wait.

Gifts

T HREE SCENES visit me like Wise Men bearing gifts in Bethlehem. I store them carefully, for they are beyond all price. I lay them before me now and hold one to the light. It is the second scene, the second gift, and it is a gift of letting go:

A minister calls from the altar, "Who will give this woman in marriage to this man?" Outside, December mimics April in this week that is both the first week of winter and the week of Christmas. A wedding guest coughs as if to cue my single line.

On my arm one of her hands is as light as a petal. A woman clothed in winter white, a woman bearing spring flowers, a woman who is still my daughter. We walked in step, in time, together down the aisle of this historic Pioneer Chapel. Beneath our feet the old floorboards creak slightly to mark our passage. We walk together like those shy, hardy girls and their sober, whiskered fathers a century ago. My own beard is gray, and the last time I walked from an altar before old friends and family I greedily took with me another man's daughter.

Those hardy farmers and daughters now long dead must

have also heard the floorboards creak in counterpoint to the organ as they neared the altar and the banked flowers. Following in the old footsteps, I feel I have rehearsed unaware this part, for we have walked before, my daughter and I, an evening or an afternoon, her small light hand in mine. We walked out into the neighborhood of our first house to view the gardens or just beyond the houses to a bluff where we could look out over the Willamette River. She was a favorite of the old folks who indulged her with flowers.

But today's flowers are not for my house, nor the young woman who waits for me to play my part and speak my line, as a proper father should. How can I give what I do not own? Have never owned. Her mother bore her. And I was but a witness with no prescribed lines in the April of her birth. Again in a mock April, a winter most mild, I stand still playing a small role again, but this time with one short line. I am a man without property here who blesses again with witness as you, my daughter, release yourself from my arm to glide the short distance to your husband-to-be, leaving me in the wake of your white gown. To myself I say, "Daughter, you and your world, you alone own." To the minister's question, I finally answer, "I will."

I hold to the light another scene and the first gift, a gift of hope:

I am not far from the Pioneer Chapel, but I am much farther back in time. I am in a small hospital that overlooks the Willamette River. It is April and dark into the night. Across the river the fishermen have formed their hog line, and their lanterns form a bridge of lights doubled by reflection. Beneath them the salmon make their spring run to breed and die above the falls. They are not quite exhausted as they pause before the falls among the baited hooks. I wait like the fishermen in the dark who pull out of the black river the flashing salmon. I wait for my wife and the baby she is delivering after a difficult pregnancy and now a hard birth.

I wait as the night reaches toward day, and alone I pray for two lives, knowing that death's hook dangles in the current of birth. There are no prescribed words, so I fall into the simple prayers of my childhood and swim through my fears with hope. My daughter slips, wet and shiny, into our time. She is her mother's creation, truth be told, and I but a man blessed only in witness, and an audience of one, or an actor with a small part in this drama and one without lines. Hope more than faith has been rewarded, and in joy and relief I see my holy family. I will call our parents, the grandfathers and grandmothers. We live on. My daughter's life is all before her.

I hold to the light a third scene and my third gift, the gift of the life:

Again it is the week of Christmas and the week of my daughter's wedding anniversary. It is my turn to wait by the phone, alone and anxious. My son-in-law calls to announce the birth of my first grandchild, a little boy of eight pounds and twenty inches. Four time zones away, he calls to say that the baby is fine but my daughter is in surgery.

There will be more calls from him and from my wife, who is by our daughter's side. My daughter is thousands of miles away; she is a woman surviving a difficult birth. I think of the baby she was and that young man I was, looking out over the Willamette. And I hope again for her life.

It is the 26th of December, the feast of the holy family. A tsunami takes its toll on the other side of the world. So much death. And we calculate the numbers. At the same time, how many babies are born? The hooks of death are always in the currents of life.

Yet they do not touch my family this holy day. I am a grandfather. We live on. My grandson's life is all before him.

III

Holy Places, Holy People:
Epiphanies of Place

Holy Places, Holy People

U NDER THE HIGH vaulted ceilings of imitation
Gothic churches in Massachusetts and New York,
I knelt before the tabernacles that were the holy places of
my youth. Before I mastered my letters, I read the lives
of holy men and women in stained glass. The schools I
attended were always near churches, and the nuns and
priests who taught me the names of the stained-glass saints
were themselves the holy people of my childhood.

Among the stories and imaginings that nurtured me
were saints' lives and picture-book renderings of shrines
and holy lands. From the lips of my parents came the stories of St. Francis and the birds, and Blessed Martin, the
biracial (though we didn't use that word then) sacristan
and apothecary, who spoke to mice and rats in faraway
Peru. Stories of wonder and miracle and sacrifice. And
I held these stories, as children do, without reflection or
question, and they were, in their way, as real as the church
and school down the street.

In childhood the closest I came to the holy places of the
stained-glass windows was the North American Martyrs'
Shrine in Auriesville, New York. There, centuries earlier,

Father Isaac Jogues and his fellow Jesuits were tortured and murdered by the Mohawks. The shrine itself is a massive circular structure built of rough-hewn logs to suggest the walls of the Mohawk encampment where the Jesuits were killed. But the grounds around the shrine have close-mown lawns and carefully maintained trails, not unlike those of a public park.

The present nearly obliterates the past at Auriesville. The smoke of the Mohawk fires, the energy of the village that once stood there, even the drama of the faith and blood remains buried; the one exception is the disinterred skeletons of the Mohawks that are displayed in the shrine's museum (or were when I visited it as a boy). Those skulls and bones held my youthful imagination fast. They were not the martyrs' bones, but I saw them in dreams as the price for sainthood. I measured faith differently thereafter: Isaac Jogues had stepped from the stained-glass window as a dark and haunting presence.

I grew and saw the world beyond the streets of my church. In college I met another haunting Jesuit. I remember the day I saw him first: I sat with other freshman by the windows of our commons watching the snow swirl in a late winter storm, and across the field that separated the commons and the priests' residence strode a thin spectral figure, erect in the wind, his black cassock and sash swirling, his head obscured by a fur-lined hood. He was gaunt and he moved with determination.

"Father Daniel Berrigan," I was told.

As I moved from class and chapel towards my degree and graduation, Berrigan moved from the same classrooms and chapels to civil rights and antiwar movements. His presence forced us to reconsider the boundaries of our faith. As a teacher, poet, priest, and prophet he challenged the authority of the walls that confined our college, country, and church. He made faith dynamic and yoked it to service and political activism. He disobeyed civil laws, allowed his poetry to drift dangerously close to propaganda, manipulated the national media like a skilled conductor, was hunted down, imprisoned, and wrote epistles from his cell. If he was saintly, he was also quite human. And his life watched from the vantage of a Catholic campus offered a new vision of chapel and classroom. In the debates that he fueled, I could see that college was not only an archive and depository for faith but also a laboratory and creative center. Faith might be recorded and preserved there, and it might also be challenged and redefined. It was a place where shadows as well as light might fall.

As I sit at my keyboard now, so many years away from my youth, I find that Berrigan has followed me in ways I never imagined and to places as improbable and fantastic as a child's bedtime story. In the glossy pages of more than one of the popular magazines where I take my idle reading, Father Berrigan smiled impishly over a bowl of Ben & Jerry's "smooth no chunks!" ice cream. He was not identified by name, but the small print informed me that if I "send ten bucks," I would in turn be sent a poster of Berrigan and the seven other social activists in the advertisement, as well as "info" about their activism. The God of my childhood still moves in wondrous and mysterious and perhaps mischievous ways.

Not entirely without coincidence, I have followed Berrigan to a life of teaching at a Catholic university, where

I often discover my epiphanies among my students. They come like grace, unexpected but always welcomed. One student was a young Navajo man who was willing to give life to a skeletal lecture about Northwest tribes that I was struggling through: He offered the analogy of his own people.

The young Navajo spoke with a quiet authority that obviously flowed from deep feeling and experience. His voice was older than his face; he spoke from a different place and a different time, toward which his cadences moved us. Briefly he was a shaman communing over a sand painting with a patient.

As a boy he had slept on the earth and watched over sheep, and time seemed generous. The land where he lived was holy, and so too were the old people, those who still dream in Navajo. His dream was to grow old on the same land. Yet here he was among us, a stranger in a strange land, learning how to deal and live with us so that he might serve his people as a bridge—or perhaps a protective wall. He was an ironic crusader, sent to protect his holy land by leaving it. He spoke sadly but without self-pity or bitterness. He could even joke about how his residence hall colleagues mistook his ritual pipe smoking for a more common misdemeanor. They were, of course, partly right, for he was truly "counter culture" in his prayers to a different God and hopes for a different life. With sadness he confessed that he had begun to dream in English. Because of his faith in the spirit of his people and their land, he sacrificed much of his life.

A class bell jarred us back to the world of minutes and books; in Navajo ritual, the sand painting would be despoiled, the picture erased, and the materials of the picture carried out and discarded. The bell despoiled the picture but could not erase it. Each of us carried away fragments, and I, for one, have held one fragment of his word-painting ever since. His young face, his wise voice, his holy words remain in my mind:

> smoke
> cloud
> rain
> acceptance
> breathing in

My young Navajo student served the present by revering the past. Both past and present were ennobled by his sacrifice, and I have come to believe that this sort of sacrifice is a powerful way of faith.

In my life I have witnessed similar sacrifices, some close to home, some at a great distance. Until her death some years ago, Dorothy Day held a place in my community (and I suspect in other communities and faiths as well) that Mother Teresa recently held. Both women are spoken of as modern saints—a designation neither sought. Both lived by faith and both prodded providence in ways that seem beyond the powers of most humans.

In the early 1930s Dorothy Day opened houses of hospitality for the destitute in New York City and began to publish *The Catholic Worker,* an epistle more than a newspaper that became her voice to the world. Over and over she would say, "Poverty is my vocation, to live simply and as poorly as I can, and to never cease talking and writing of poverty and destitution. Here and everywhere." By the power of her prayer and the press she addressed and alleviated poverty for over half a century, and she died a deservedly venerated woman.

I never met Dorothy Day, though I was deeply touched by her presence once—not in New York but at Marquette University in Wisconsin. One day on that campus I paused in a Gothic chapel dedicated to St. Joan of Arc. The granite chapel is a fourteenth-century treasure, painstakingly transported and reassembled from the French village of Chasse. It was a small building, solid and intimate. If you bow your head before its altars, the multi-colored light that passes through century-old mullions bathes you in the past. A few steps from the chapel, in the hermetically sealed seclusion of the university archives, an archivist spread Dorothy Day's letters, journals, and manuscripts on long wooden tables and I bowed my head to read.

Her words touched me much as the little chapel had, because both carried the past boldly into the present. Dorothy Day's faith in providence, her belief that Christ could and should be found in all people—no matter how destitute or wayward—and her work as a social activist all had root in her nearly literal response to the gospel. Her life and her work had medieval patterns. Her houses of hospitality (shelters for the poor, the alcoholic, the abused) and her writings in *The Catholic Worker* sprang from a belief in communal living. Her shelters were a modern equivalent of the monasteries that were hospital, home, and sanctuary in the distant past. She went into the streets with open hands to care for the needy and depended on the goodwill of her neighbors and providence to provide her with the means to extend her work. Her faith was so deep that both answered. And like the granite chapel of St. Joan, which was both anachronistic and beautifully set among the brick and glass halls of Marquette, Dorothy Day's faith remains a beautiful if discordant note in the modern world.

In her life of poverty she allowed herself two indulgences, two simple pleasures: reading and music. Her columns in *The Catholic Worker* represented one kind of testimony, but I found another testimony in her daybooks and journals. They revealed that this extraordinary faith lived in a very ordinary woman. In a 1943 notebook, after a recipe for bread making, Dorothy has a list of things "to learn":

> meditate,
> sing,
> canning,
> cheese,
> honey extracting,
> kill duck,
> save feathers.

At the same time that she wrote these things she was attempting to found communal centers that could be self-sufficient in all areas. "Save feathers": The scrap of paper with these words deserves its place in the archives. Too often we see faith as heavenly, but faith is of this earth, nourished by people who wish to learn to sing.

I have flowed with a great throng of faithful through massive *torii* during the Oban festivals in Japan. I have washed my hands in the purification troughs and carried from the temples and shrines the odor of incense, the smoke of sandalwood. I've seen the faces of Japan, young and old, rich and poor, at prayer. I've happened upon little temples and shrines in the midst of skyscrapers, places as old as the reassembled chapel of St. Joan. I've heard the gong of a temple bell and listened while Buddhist monks chanted; the sounds were not as foreign as I imagined they would be. I've watched an old and plain-faced Buddhist nun happily give away her only food, trusting providence would provide more. And I have been tempted to heresy: to distrust the walls of all religions, even my own, when the stones of practice seem set against the life of faith. I am uncomfortable with anyone who preaches the one true faith. In the name of faith many lives have been taken as well as given.

Once I traveled to an English plain and walked to a university town within medieval walls. By candlelight I sat with dons and students in an ancient hall and enjoyed centuries-old traditions. On that same wide plain I visited a cathedral, also centuries old. As so many others, I stood in awe at what faith could build in stone and glass; yet the glass spoke more deeply of faith than I had expected. Huge sections of windows that once had been stained were glazed in clear panes that reminded me of the bleached windows of old warehouses. German bombing during the Second World War had destroyed some of the panels, but stones and bullets, thrown in religious struggles, had shattered others. This cathedral had alternately housed Catholics and Protestants through the years; depending on the era, it could have been as dangerous a place for either faith as a Mohawk village once was for a Jesuit missionary.

I do not like the thought of those blank windows. I prefer to think of the light of faith falling in colors as it did in the churches of my childhood. The blank windows lodge in my memory like glass scars. But there is solace in the notion that time heals all wounds, even those of faith.

There is a sign of this healing on my own campus. Three days a week I teach a class held in the basement of one of the oldest buildings at the university. The floor above my class is composed mostly of students' residence rooms, but there is also a Catholic chapel with stained-glass windows. In the basement, across from my classroom, there is an Islamic prayer room. It is a humble structure, a bit shabby, but faith and learning grow there in tolerance and respect. I believe holiness touches such a place, touches the people who study and pray there; just as holiness touched the church walls and stained-glass windows of my childhood, and the students, clergy, and living saints and students I have known. Perhaps from the right vantage any life is a journey filled with holy people and holy places.

The Poetry of Silence

M Y OWN JOURNEY to holy places has been through churches, libraries, classrooms, and the out-of-doors. I think of a church first and the power of its silence as well as its words. In remembering, words and silence paradoxically merge. From the start I fumbled with silence as much as my first Latin responses as an altar boy at Mass: *Ad Deum qui laetificat juventutem meam,* to God, the joy of my youth. God held me differently in the joy of my youth when Latin was a sound rather than a language and my serving more a matter of rote than liturgy. The young curate must have learned patience teaching us to pronounce clearly and to wait between responses. His instruction, like that of my parents, the nuns at school, my coach at the YMCA, seemed to emphasize the spoken; but the subtext of serving, of youth itself, was appreciating silence.

The shushing finger to the lips, the sentence of quiet time in the corner, the pulled ear, the nun's ruler across the knuckles, and the walk to the end of the team bench: These were the dramatic instructions. But it was the silence about silence that revealed the most. Stepping from the sacristy to the altar, the priest seemed to wear another vestment, as did my parents when they took their place in the pew. I learned early that silence was not necessarily quietness, the absence of sound, but only a movement toward the quiet. At the most sacred moments the pipes clang, someone coughs, a stomach rumbles. Silence is willed and projected into the unceasing noise of the world.

My father used silence almost as a tool. He took me to woods and fields when I was very young. And I remember riding on his shoulder, most likely on the way home when my interest flagged and my legs could not keep up with his. From those outings I retain memories too of a conspiratorial silence as we caught sight of a bird or animal partially visible among the branches of trees or in the hillocks of a field. So many walks and so many years ago, the sightings now merge: pheasants, woodchucks, killdeer, and deer. My father had gone to the woods as a hunter, though he put aside his gun as a youth; he then became an artist and so he brought to the wild the sharp eyes of both vocations. So I walked by his side mimicking his silence and concentration.

I never took up my father's gun or palette, but years later I would haunt wild places myself, and I tried to hone the skills of watching and stalking that he shared in few words. By nature he was a talker, a natural lecturer, and I think it was only in the woods, museums, and churches that silence seemed natural for him. On my solitary rambles I took delight in moving quietly, open to every sound around me. And if I listened carefully, I *saw* more: in winter a field mouse outside of his tunnel runs; in spring, the first of migratory birds; in summer, a velvet brown mourning cloak butterfly basking against the dark brown skin of an oak. Part of my pleasure was to get close enough to take a sort of coup, like the plains Indians who often would ride close enough to tag their enemy. But only insects would let me that close.

Later I would learn that there were powerful silences indoors, too, in the homes and classroom where I spent my days. When I was new to teaching, I scored the notes, acts, movements within a class, and I have thought of silence as a large unit between acts, or sometimes as an extended set piece. Silence is necessary even before the class: The student studies, the teacher prepares the lesson; and these parallel acts, carried out in silence or in the white noise of music, are themselves a kind of silence. Examinations, too, wear a cloak of silence, the silence in that case symbolizing seriousness, integrity, and concentration. I have closed my eyes as my students filled out their blue examination books and thought the quiet (punctuated by suppressed coughs and the turning of pages) not unlike the quiet passages of communal liturgies.

The conductor and composer Leonard Bernstein was often in search of the silence between notes, and I find those silences between the words that are the score of a class. I sometimes play a successful class back in my mind, slowly listening for the silences where insight and discovery sparked to life. And I play back not only the classes I teach but also the classes in which I was taught. I hear the teacher's voice, asking students to consider a line, a passage, and the hypothesis of a lecture. There is a pause while eyes turn to the book, while minds turn to the idea;

in such pauses light shines. Or there is the pause after an unexpected question. In those silent pauses insight may emerge. The mind grapples, puzzles, grasps, and discovers. A class may move by fits and starts with as much energy expended in the pauses as in the spoken exchanges. An exact transcript of the spoken words would be an incomplete record of what went on, like a play script with the occasional note for "pause" or "long pause." In life, as in art, so much may be said in silence.

For all its importance we do not speak much about silence, though it may touch our lives with as much pleasure or pain as words. When we were young, we could hurl the lines "sticks and stones will break my bones, but words will never hurt me" at the words that really did hurt. There is so much love and so much hurt in words, but the same is true of silence.

And we are surely as attuned to the *rhetoric* of silence as we are to words. There are conventions. I listened one fall to the young writer Terry Tempest Williams read from her work to a large audience on our campus. At the end of her reading (at what might have been, in fact, the end of her reading) she bowed her head in silence. At first it was a dramatic and effective gesture; her concerns had been serious and moving. But she held the silence beyond the seconds one would expect, and the added seconds of silence began to burden some in the lecture hall. The pause was as provocative as anything she said. And I realized silence might be as nuanced as sound.

In the churches where I served as an altar boy, the murals and Stations of the Cross suggested distinctive silences: 40 days in the desert, the agony in the garden, the death on the cross, the silent tableaux of the Nativity, forever intertwined in my memory with the singing of "Silent Night." Silence means many things, not all of them holy. Yet silence allows an Advent, the sight of the bird amid branches, a bow at the foot of the altar.

Tongues of Fire

WHEN I LOOKED to those altars as a child, I
watched the flickering of the candles, the holy
fire. Their flickering still catches me and rekindles a host
of memories. In Catholic churches, a celebrant strikes the
year's new fire after dark on the Saturday before Easter. In
my altar boy youth, I also ignited a great fire—this one on
Palm Sunday.

I had served at an early Mass where my duties included
the lighting and extinguishing of candles; one of the privi-
leges of altar-boying was Keeper of the Flame. I brought
new waxy palm fronds home and took the old papery
ones from behind the house's crucifixes. While my father
shaved and mother and brothers dressed, I took on the
sacred task of burning the old palms; blessed by a priest's
hand, they could not be simply tossed away. I chose the
side of our garage and to thwart a breeze resorted to burning the palms in a cardboard box. The task took the entire
handful of wooden matches I requisitioned from the box
my mother dipped into when she had to light the pilot of
our gas stove or table candles.

The palms shriveled to vague ashes that I left in the box.

I went inside. The breezed stoked the ashes, the ashes ignited the cardboard box, and the box ignited the garage. Discovery and alarm had no effect on my churchgoing family, who dismissed it as one of my pranks. My father, in fact, never put his Gillette down. A garden hose and an alert neighbor who called the fire department saved most of the garage, the family car, and me. Actually my father got the worst of it; my mother defended me on the principle of my religious intent and judged him guilty of ignoring a son's plea for help. It didn't matter; the unchecked fire had terrified me more than any punishment my father might have devised.

Like so much else in my first years, I watched my first destructive fire while sitting on his shoulder. A junkyard by the Housatonic River, which meandered through our town, burnt down one summer night, and all the other fires I've seen since rekindle those first images. I can still hear the crackle and see the two fires, the one blazing on land, the other eerily reflected on the surface of the very water the firemen were pumping into their hoses.

Those garage and the junkyard fires were exceptional; in general the flames that flickered in my youth were benign. Yet there seemed to be more fire in my past than now. Perhaps I just spent more time in church, often with a candle or censer in my hand, measuring my growth by my ability to light the tall candles. Outdoors in New England and later in Portland, the almost-sweet tobacco-ish whiff of burning leaves drifted through most neighborhoods on sunny Saturdays and Sundays after the first frost but before the first snow. Before I took on the chore of burning the leaves by myself, I helped my father rake

The Play of Light

the leaves into piles that we carried in bushel baskets to a bare spot in the backyard or near the end of the driveway. The leaves burnt from below, and to keep the fire going my father would lift the corner of a pile with his rake. The flames would leap out and lick the air like the garter snakes we sometimes surprised while weeding my mother's rock garden. It is long ago that my father let me light the leaves for the first time, and no one burns leaves in the city now.

Ulcers, my mother, and a determined GP took my father's tobacco away before I was born, but he kept his favorite pipes. Mimicking movie actors, I stood before the hall mirror trying to hold a borrowed meerschaum at the proper angle in the grip of my baby teeth. I didn't like the taste of the stem at first or the stale odor of the charred bowl, but there was the hint of burning leaves in both. By the time I had affected the uniforms of writers and professors—tweeds and a pipe—my father had given his briars away. So I stood before the same mirror puffing at my own pipe, recovering a bit of past falls in the smoke that I artfully exhaled in my best authorial dust-jacket pose.

Hindsight may rightly judge the smoky seminars of the sixties and seventies as unhealthy, and the thought now of teaching in a room of smoke strikes me as incongruous; I am after clarity, after all. Yet I took notes and later lectured across tables bearing the circles of Styrofoam coffee cups and ashtrays filled with filters, nubs, and the blackened wood matches of the pipe smoker. We breathed the air of coffeehouse, pub, and hotel bar of the writers we read and debated. Struck matches and the rituals of lighting up punctuated the rounds of our talk, flames bursting among our humble epiphanies. Fire, talk, and smoke: at the time the combination seemed as old and as unquestioned as prayer and incense. On the top of my office bookshelves, I have a holder with six pipes, not smoked for more years than I want to count. They smell like my father's old pipes, and there is a hint of leaf fire in their scent.

I teach in a fluorescent world now, but I have seen many photographs of our gaslit classrooms in the not-too-distant past, and *burning the midnight oil* and *lighting a candle at both ends* were not always exam-week clichés. Flames flickered above the first students at most universities, flames that are mostly hidden now: our various boilers, furnaces, and stoves hide their fire and shield their pilot lights from view. In the quiet shadows of the campus chapels the sanctuary lights remain as the only constant lambent flames. Our campus chaplain calls them "God's porch lights."

I have seen similar flames in Japanese shrines and temples, and have no doubt holy fires burn round the globe. But the sanctuary candles are the flames I grew up with, and if the primitive cooking and warming fires inevitably succumb, as they must, to a fluorescent world, I like the notion of those sanctuary candles flickering in the shadows of the future as beacons of where we have been and where we might go.

The Play of Light

Clay and Wood, Stone and Bone

A BOVE THE ALTAR CANDLES in those churches of
my childhood hung crucifixes, and statues looked
down from the side altars. To grow up Catholic is to grow
up among statues and figurines. It is a fact of my life I take
for granted, much as I might take the presence of trees
here in the Northwest. A non-Catholic colleague whose
tolerance and faith I admire raised an eyebrow at the sta-
tus of statues in our churches; his raised eyebrow was a
gentle question, and it made me think.

Over my office door there is a bronze crucifix that lay
once on my mother's coffin. In my home there is a crucifix
hung by our front door that was a wedding present of a
priest who watched over me as I grew up. In almost every
classroom where I teach similar crucifixes look down from
the walls. Every January as the new year opens, the chore
list I have clipped by my computer includes a note "to
take down tree and decorations," which means, in part,
that I must pack away the manger and the angel that tops
our tree. In the spring, in many parts of the Catholic
world, flowers will be placed before the statues of Mary,
the Blessed Mother. This is a seasonal ritual for me and for

many, but it is an odd if inexplicable practice, I suppose, to an outsider.

I have no memory of a first recognition: the crucifixes, manger, and statues of Mary preceded my arrival much as trees have. They were givens. It was years before I thought of the ugly physical implications of the crucifix, and only recently have I really enjoyed the irony and diversity of my family's nativity figures, a haphazard collection gathered over time and in different places. A few of the figures were made in Italy, and the rest in countries where the artisans were most likely Buddhists. What did they think of the artifacts they were making?

I cannot claim to remember the statuary of the baptismal font where I was officially greeted into the Church, but I do have memories of Church statues. Since the adults around me blocked my vision of the liturgy proper, I responded to the music and to the statues and carvings visible above the adults who towered above me. Even before I could tell time by a watch, I knew where we were in the Mass by the music, and I do not think anyone beside the sculptors and carvers knew the statuary better than I did. I made up stories to explain those wood, granite, and plaster faces. I was doing things backwards, of course, since the statues were based on history or tradition—stories already written. But my stories and my emotional responses to the statues and music were not all that off the mark, and I think I had the themes right.

In some of the churches the statues were actually works of art; in others, the plaster figures were vulgar if not grotesque, but lighting, thank God, was often equally deficient, a situation that gave my imagination free rein to interpret or respond to the shadowed figures. I was drawn then, as I still am, to the unnamed figures: the trumpeting angels carved in the pulpit, the caryatids, the soldiers and observers in the background of the Stations of the Cross, and the shepherds in the nativity scene. They seemed real people. I had my favorites; some visages frightened me. They were not unlike the adults around me whom I also stole peeks at when they were momentarily in prayer (or what I interpreted then as prayer). So early on I linked the world of statues and the world of people.

But I did not confuse the two; one was not the other; and like my non-Catholic colleague I too raised an eyebrow at the mere hint of idolatry and superstition. No religion with statuary seems immune; the desperate and ignorant are prone to misusing the symbolic. So are the powerful. So it is. The wellspring of sculpture and religion may flow from a common source, perhaps, and our distinctions of high art, folk art, liturgical art, and popular art are recent in the long view of humanity. It is through statues and drawings, among other things, that we attempt to peer back into the long history.

But I do not find statues in themselves particularly mysterious. I can pop into the university art room on any afternoon and watch students molding clay statues, and my own children grew up with "play dough" and clay as well as crayons and finger paint. We have always liked to tell silent stories in clay or wood or stone or bone, stories that travel well in time, stories that one can literally walk around, that one can touch. In the oldest story of my culture, God fashions us from spittle and clay and bone. And ever since, we have fashioned similarly what we love or what we wish to know.

Except for my years at graduate school, I have always studied or worked in buildings where crucifixes hung or where statues and shrines dotted the campus. Even at that graduate school, I had the benefit of the work of Ivan Mestrovic, who had been a resident sculptor there. I had a special fondness for his larger-than-life Job, who greeted me in all kinds of weather, enduring snow, ice, rain, and blazing sun. I could run my fingers over the knotted muscle, feel as the sculptor did the long sharp line of the shinbone, and watch the light play over the resigned eyes. Job was always and never the same. In the curl of the toes or the bending of a finger pulsed the patience and the pity and the beauty of humanity.

On the wall above my kitchen table, I have a small wooden statue of St. Francis carved by my artist father when he was a boy. It is a simple statue, very brown with age. The face is nearly unfinished, in the hands on the breast a clutched bird, on the feet sandals. Like all good sculpture, it honors the humble human body. Simple as the statue is, it holds for me not only the tangible link with my father but also the tensions within my church whose words so often enunciate a distrust of the body and whose sculpture, painting, and song so often celebrate and worship through the body.

Today I will most certainly pass by the *crucerios* that stands among a grove of redwoods at a campus crossroads (paths to be exact). The roots of the trees have given the granite cross a slight tilt toward the morning sun, and mushrooms sprout up among the brown needles around its base.

I find it a holy place and am moved by the simply carved

figure of St. James, whose eyes are nearly level with my own. Like so many side altars where I have knelt in my life, it is a prayerful and holy place: The rhythm of stone, not unlike that of words and music, may dispose the mind to reflect and pray. At their best the artistic and the spiritual meet at a crossroads, and one can travel either way to the same destination.

———

I have always felt most at home near the side altars where silence, candles, and statuary invite peace and prayer, especially those altars where a statue of Mary shadows my prayers. Somewhere in the labyrinth of grammar school religious instruction, one of our patient nuns spent considerable time explaining the role of Mary as an intercessor, illustrating the point with the story of the marriage feast and the miracle of water changed to wine.

I wasn't quite sure at the time what to make of the concept. Was I to take my prayers up the side altar? Put in a word with the Mother before tackling the Son? But as a son myself, I knew mothers had the say. The analogy would have worked for me if Mary were interceding with Joseph, who seemed to my boyish mind to be and not to be like my father. I kept (wisely perhaps) that confusion to myself; it didn't matter. Then and now my perceptions of Mary have never been dogmatic. Instead a whole complex of emotions has grown from stories, and the pictures and statues in my home and church have been the illustrations of those stories.

As a child (and even now) setting up the Christmas manger kindled deep feelings, especially reverence for the

The Play of Light

power and beauty of the maternal and feminine that held my child's world together. I remember placing the blue-robed figurine of Mary into the straw, and it was large in my small hand. This past year, I joined the parish work party that sets up our crèche in front of the side altar. It involved removing the nearly life-size statue of Mary from the altar and assembling a rather large stable of fir boughs. When I carried the nativity scene up from the cellar closet where the figurines wait each year in darkness before advent, I needed two hands. It was as if the proportions of my childhood had returned. And when two of us carried the larger statue off to the sacristy, I noticed that a finger and the palm of one hand were damaged. Silver wires of the armature protruded from a ragged gap in the plaster; it struck me as a kind of wound. It broke the spell of its artistic illusion. It also echoed a story I read in my teens.

In the story by Giovanni Guareschi, a good-hearted but wily pastor of an impoverished parish loathes the centuries-old and ugly terra cotta statue of the Madonna venerated by his faithful little flock. When the pastor, Don Camillo, finds a crack in it, he goes against the advice of his conscience (which speaks to him from the altar crucifix) and changes the annual procession route so that the statue will be driven on a truck bed over the town's roughest roads. Like Guareschi's Don Camillo, I loathe ugly statues. My artist father, a devout Catholic with a gift for restoration, passed on to me a distrust of statues poorly created or poorly used. These statues I would gladly fling on the Italian pastor's flatbed though I could not expect the same result. In the story, the statue cracks further and splits apart to reveal a silver Madonna hidden centuries ago under the covering of ugly clay.

A treasure, however, lies within many statues, not silver perhaps, but the glimpse of something real and profound held in terra cotta or painted plaster. As in a painting or story, the illusion of reality is necessary to catch the truth of reality. There are times when the poor light and humble statues of side aisles conspire to give body to the woman growing from the young mother of the nativity into the sorrowful mother at the foot of the cross. In her arms Mary holds life and death. There are, of course, the beautiful statues also: Michelangelo's "Pietà" or Mestrovic's "Virgin and Child" or the almost haunting "Madonna and Child" of the Jewish sculptor Jacob Epstein. And humble or magnificent, statues grow in beauty and power from what successive views bring and take from them.

This summer during a renovation of my church, the statues were taken from the altars to the church basement, Mary with the broken hand among them. I did not inherit my father's artistic skill, but I have his tools and sat by his side often enough as a boy while he worked at restoration to be able to repair the broken hand. I felt like Don Camillo, though our means were opposite. He unveiled the treasure of his statue by destroying its shell. I like to think that with spatula and brush I protected our treasure, giving it back its shell of illusion, so that Mary reaches out as she has for generations to those who come to her in the shadows of the side aisle.

Wise in Stories

A CHURCH, as a holy place, offers the silence of space
and light and art, but it is also a place of words and
music and people. There are the words of ritual based
on our oldest cherished stories. There are the preachers'
homilies, today's stories. And there are the stories we tell
each other.

After Mass, I sat one Sunday morning in the church
basement with an older Mexican woman who always kneels
in the pew behind me. She was deep in conversation with
a younger man, but they abandoned Spanish to include
me when I approached with my usual tea and donut. We
talked as people do who have first met, and the talk led us
to a subject we both had in common: young people.

The man expressed sadness at the plight of young im-
migrants who had forsaken family and at the despair of
families who had lost young men to drugs and violence.
He had a story he wanted to share with these young men,
perhaps as a guest speaker in schools, but he was uneasy
about how to tell it. As a teacher of literature and writing,
would I give him advice? Would I listen to his story?

"A young woman was poor, and because she was poor

she went with many men. And when she became pregnant, she worried about what would happen to her and to the child. The time came and she gave birth alone in the dark, and knowing she could not give the child a home, she left it among the tall canes in a field between two farms.

"Another young woman, one of three daughters who lived with their widowed mother, walked the road by the cane field the next day. As she walked she thought she heard a baby cry, but she was afraid to go alone deep in the canes. She stopped at the farm, and they told her not there nor at the neighboring farm was there an infant. It was a bird perhaps; in the cane their cries sounded almost human. On her way back, she heard the cries again; she told her mother and they returned with a man from the neighborhood to search among the canes.

"They found the infant swaddled in a thin blanket and covered in its excrement. Ants had nibbled away the skin from its nose and eyelids and ears. It was weak. One of the sisters worked in a pharmacy, and in that country the pharmacist would also be the doctor. They brought him the baby. He gave them medicine but no hope. The child would most likely die. The four women cared for it day and night. They prayed. The baby lived. Wounds healed. In the house of women, a little boy found a family.

"In turn each of the girls found a husband and left their mother's house. With each marriage the little boy acquired two new families: the sister and her husband, and also the husband's family. Eventually the boy had seven families. They all raised him. When he was old enough, he lived alone until the mother grew old and infirm and he returned to take care of her until she died. . . ."

Before the story reached the death of the mother, I had already searched the storyteller's face, looking for scars on his eyelids and nose. This was his story.

He wondered how the story would touch young people, especially the ones drifting from the ties of family. He wanted to share the power of simple love and the respect it deserves. What should he do with the story?

"Tell it," I told him.

I walked from the pew where I had heard the Gospel and homily to folding chairs where I listened to a story from South America. I will retell the story. I thought of all the men who have spoken to me from the altar and the pulpit, telling and retelling stories. It is a thought I shared with an old friend from Italy. Bruna poured me a glass of wine, and at her kitchen table we exchanged stories, a ritual we repeat every couple of weeks. A priest brought us together, and many of our stories are about him or the other priests who entered our lives, usually for the better. She tells me about growing up in Italy; I tell her about growing up in New England.

She is, by far, the better storyteller, and one of my favorite stories has to do with a popular assistant pastor who she said brewed more than a few bottles of grappa in the church basement. This was technically illegal but overlooked by most of the parishioners, many of whom shared the rewards of the good Father's labor. Out of envy, a brother priest turned him in to the appropriate agency, which did not press charges, but did, to the sorrow of many in the parish, pour the grappa into the church's storm drain. In the following week, church neighbors and their cats noticed

rather bemused rats emerging from the sewers and wander-
ing nearby streets in loopy circles.

In exchange for her story, I told her about the first
priest that I clearly remembered, a distant cousin of my
mother who was a young priest when she was a girl. He
was also one of the assistant pastors in the church across
the street from my childhood home. And my memory is
not of his pastoral acumen or his spirituality, though I
imagine he possessed both. What I remember is that he
frightened me, perhaps because he was older than my parents and gruff under bushy eyebrows, or perhaps because
he was undoubtedly a special ward of St. Christopher, who
in those days was still an accredited patron of travelers.

His habit was to reach into the collection bag while
driving back from the Sunday Mass he had said at a mission
church, to pull out a fifty-cent piece as a reward for the
altar boy who accompanied him. He would usually do
this while driving over a narrow bridge. Fifty-cent pieces
sunk to the bottom of the moneybag, so in trying to drive
with one hand and fish out the coin with the other, he
slalomed dangerously down the road. My nine-year-old
life flashed before me each time he fumbled with the bag,
and I'm sure he put the fear of the Lord into every other
driver who happened to be coming our way.

Then Bruna told me about an uncle of hers in Italy
who had fallen away from the Church for many years.
One night when she was young, she heard pebbles strike
her window. It was her uncle, begging her to immediately
intercede with Dom Angelo so that the uncle could make
a good confession immediately. He thought Dom would

honor the request of good child. So they threw pebbles at Dom Angelo's window, and he woke, heard the request, and then opened the church to hear the sinner's confession. He went back to bed.

Halfway home after his confession the uncle pleaded with Bruna to take him right back to the rectory, for he felt the need for communion immediately. Again the pebbles at the priest's window, again Dom Angelo opened the church.

Later that day the uncle died of a heart attack.

We tell these priest stories from the outside, but recently I've had a glimpse of their lives from the inside. In a parish desperate for volunteers, I signed up to visit the sick, envisioning this as time spent cheering up shut-ins with stories. Instead my pastor asked me to bring communion to the dying. When I protested that as a recovering Catholic (at best) I was an especially unworthy choice, he said simply that none of us are worthy. So in the weeks before she died, I brought communion to a single mother who lived in a public housing complex with her nine-year-old son. Life had not been especially good to her. She had withered like an old woman, and her voice was worn to a whisper. At each visit she greeted me with a formality and gratitude so sincere that I found them painful. My coming was a matter of life and death, and whether I was impostor or proxy didn't concern her; what I carried did. Faith and death were her immediate ministers.

I was humbled and troubled in the face of such belief, and found great comfort in my pastor's confession that he too learned more about faith from those he was supposed to be leading.

Not long ago, I sat with Bruna, this time at her dining-

The Play of Light

room table and with the priest who had introduced us. He was taking a vacation from his parish and the prison where he ministers. We talked of priests: of the old days, when tight-fisted pastors locked refrigerators lest their young curates raid them, and the whiskey priests who soldiered on as best they could through their loneliness and frailty, and the priests who failed. We talked of saints and sinners then, and how the distinction between the two sometimes depended on the storyteller.

Our stories told, we shared a Mass, we three aging friends, on the feast of Saint Anthony. The room was silent and Bruna had placed a crucifix and the bread and wine on the table. Three of us had gathered, and the simple, everyday room became our holy place. Father handed me the missal to do the first reading, words from Saint Paul, who seemed to have waited on the page to join us: "We hold this treasure in earthen vessels, that the surpassing power of God may be of God and not from us."

IV

Circles of Love:
Epiphanies of Childhood

Reading Hands

P ERHAPS THE OLDEST THINGS I own that are entirely mine are memories of childhood. Certainly I
have been protective of those memories. Many of them
now seem more vivid than ever. I suppose a psychologist
would tell me that as I grow older, my brain necessarily
discards and condenses memories so that I am not over-
whelmed by my past. Much as I marvel at the efficiency
and mysterious complexity of the chemical and electrical
processes that manage this, I also marvel at the mystery of
self-creation that guides us as we record and edit the ongoing story of our life. And as any good writer knows, you
have to begin the story well. The likely model is biblical:
childhood as a Garden of Eden.

Gardens are, in fact, among my earliest recollections.
They tend to merge into one garden, one replete with serpent, tree, and forbidden fruit. Not an apple or the tree of
knowledge but raspberries and a rather misshapen white
pine; not the serpent Satan but a resident garter snake. God
did not walk in that garden; my mother did. And it was she
who forbade the picking of the raspberries or tomatoes before they were ripe, and it was she who forbade the climbing

of the pitch-sticky pine. Commandments certainly broken, but I was not cast out. And in time my mother gave me two brothers to share the garden and its chores, which at the time I often resented. Raking leaves or picking berries or knocking Japanese beetles from my mother's beloved peonies into a coffee can spiked with rubbing alcohol: these struck me as cruel and unusual punishment, forcing me to pause from my headlong rush to grow up or from my callow boredom. I eased the pain, once my body settled into a picking or raking rhythm, by letting my mind pick and rake also. I have a real garden of my own now with a long row of raspberries, and I have autumn leaves to rake; still I return to that old garden in and out of season.

What I pick or rake there depends on the calendar of the seasons or providence. In the garden of memory, surprise blooms as often as expectation. All seasons are now somewhat autumnal for me, and I am more conscious of tidying and putting up my preserves than planting and weeding. But I catch myself wondering as I did so long ago when the small world that I inhabited was so immense. The larger world that I have traveled since has become much smaller. The poet Wordsworth felt that "heaven lies about us in our infancy." Very well it might, but as the poet himself celebrated, so too does the world, startling us when we are young with its everyday catalogue of wonders. At the beginning, and I believe at the end, we struggle to focus, struggling through our bodies to find our place in the world. I look to my hand, which so long ago first reached out to my mother and the world she gave me.

My artist father, who sometimes tutored promising youths, had a favorite exercise in which he required his pupils to sketch their own right hands from memory (no peeking allowed). He took the notion of knowing thyself literally. What kind of an eye, he asked, did a would-be artist have who failed to observe his most valued tool, and know its character as well as its anatomy?

I hold out my right hand for inspection, and note with some pride the calluses on my palm from garden and workshop—symbols that camouflage my sedentary life as a professor. There are white scars on fingers from childhood cuts, the most prominent from a broken bottle among rocks my brother and I gripped to pull ourselves along in the shallows before we learned to swim. My blood was so red on that small hand, whitened by the cold lake water. I never imagined then the prominent veins and hints of discoloration now. I never imagined the small hand that my father bandaged would someday become a hand like his.

My fingers also bear ink stains, from long sessions this morning correcting student papers, on which I still scrawl nearly indecipherable encouragements and cautions in longhand. *Longhand, by hand*—I relish the sound of the phrases, and the implication that I touch my students' papers as my professors touched mine. Though I agonize and complain at the sight of every new batch of student essays or blue books, I secretly rue the day technology displaces this process. The ink stains on my hands are badges of sorts, marks of the connection to that long past of things written and read.

Despite its playful blasphemy with history and literature, the much-acclaimed movie *Shakespeare in Love* had among its gospel of colorful details young Will's ink-stained fingers. That scene prompted me to ask my own students to imagine the *physical* effort that went into writing all those plays and sonnets, the cramp and ache accompanying the man's genius and imagination. I note that we have in Shakespeare's own hand only his signature. Did that unique treasure come to us from his right hand or his left?

I remind my students that so many of the greats, past and present, have burnt the proverbial midnight oil when they were near or just into their twenties, and bent over their pens then and keyboards now in the unconscious teaming of mind and hands. Labors of love often, but always manual labor. So much depends on the hands.

Yet that yoking of mind and hand has never been absolute—even as my mind searches for the next word this morning, my right hand, unwilled, strokes my beard or traces the creases in my trousers. It waits impatiently as if it has a life of its own. I suppose one of our first great tasks is controlling the hands that wave before our eyes like branches in a wind when we are infants. The ability to reach and grasp, the mastery of the spoon, the art of tying one's own shoes, writing letters and then words and then thoughts: consider the effort we invested in all of these, long ago. And still the hand is not always a faithful and obedient servant. Like the face or eyes it may mirror the soul rather than the mind, revealing, perhaps, more than the mind would wish to reveal.

Rodin, the iconoclastic French sculptor, modeled hundreds of hands, individual studies and sketches that appear to be fragments but which often possess an emotional power that allows them to stand as complete statues. Could I sketch or model the living hands that have struck me with the same beauty and power, I too might have a studio crammed with studies of hands.

I see in that studio of mine the careful fingers of my doctor, in whose hands I have literally trusted my life. They are scrubbed and gentle and skilled. Their touch is practiced and sure. Oddly the touch reminds me of my Korean *taekwondo* master from years ago, whose callused knuckles and hardened fingers were equally skilled in a very different art. Yet as he walked among us as we practiced our forms, he would correct our stances by taking our hands in his own, angling them to the right position with the deft touch of a physician.

I see my father's hand, holding a pencil, and my mother's hands, those dear hands I remember feeling more than seeing. I see the priest's hand in blessing after confession, the two raised fingers tracing a cross in the air and waving away the weight of my guilt. I see the hands of my children, the hands I have perhaps followed more closely than any others. I see, in too many ways to describe, the hand I asked for in marriage. I look at my own hand again. Not a carpenter's hand, not a mechanic's, not a surgeon's, not a farmer's, or a musician's. It is a teacher's hand, sometimes a writer's hand. I correct papers, scribble on blackboards, compose lecture notes, send off recommendations, write marginalia, gesticulate to excite classes, point to raised and expectant young hands to take a question. I steal the odd moment to try to practice the writing I teach. And I muse sometimes about endnotes, not with morbidity but with a kind of detached curiosity. What will be? What will cease to be? There will be a last class, a last paper to correct, and perhaps a last, brief poem. And this hand that has served me so well will write a last word.

A Pear Tree

B UT NOT THIS DAY when my mind drifts back to childhood and my fingers save what they can, dutifully now touching the keyboard of remembrance. I think back again, teasing out memories of the old days and of the forbidden pine tree and the other trees in the garden of my youth. I think too of the trees and garden that I now possess. My mind snatches at a song rather than painting a picture. "And a partridge in a pear tree." I am a reluctant and ungifted singer but still susceptible to a musical phrase. That pear tree with its partridge haunts me year round when I think of trees, and I find myself humming and even singing the words when there is no Christmas association at all.

Like everyone else, I first heard the words for "The Twelve Days of Christmas" during some long-ago-forgotten Christmas season, but they did not attach themselves to my memory the way other carols have. "Silent Night," especially when I hear it sung by a congregation in a full church on Christmas Eve, can bring tears to my eyes, and "Jingle Bells" carries always the joyful bustle of yuletide. If anything, I found the alliterative

The Play of Light

refrain of "partridge" and "pear" slightly annoying (hence memorable) and ridiculous, since my experiences with partridges and their cousin pheasants always involved a rush of adrenaline as their bursts into flight from ground cover scared the hell out of me. I do not imagine them in trees; turtledoves yes, partridges no.

And true love or not, I would not find a bird a particularly treasured present, but a tree is another matter. A tree, even to my younger imagination, seemed a most extraordinary and extravagant gift, especially if it were large enough for a perching partridge. For though I am not a tree hugger, I am assuredly a lover of trees. For half my life, I've mostly enjoyed other people's trees like the poet in Thoreau's *Walden* who "enjoyed the most valuable part of a farm, while the crusty farmer supposed he had got a few apples only." A bit west of Walden I sneaked into orchards for the climbing rather than the fruit, and in legion with other scamps played cowboys and Indians (unimaginable now) or soldiers, using the trees as our stage for whatever Saturday afternoon film we were reenacting.

The family yard had two trees: the ungainly pitch pine and a stately elm that dwarfed our two-story house. The garage and the pine I nearly burned down while disposing of a previous year's blessed palms. I imagine the next owners removed the scorched pine, and I fear the elm fell to the Dutch elm disease that altered the look of the New England of my childhood. I don't especially regret the passing of the pine; it was too sticky to climb anyway. But the elm threw more than a massive shadow over my childhood home. It was a tree of knowledge and I was free to take from it whatever I wished.

Annual cicada nymphs crawled up from their earthen burrows each summer onto the elm's bark, and I watched them perch and pulse until the skin split on their backs, allowing each translucent winged adult to emerge and dry out on the shell of its former life. Solving the mystery of that metamorphosis sent me to the library and began a complicated metamorphosis of my own that would one day take me to the byways of nature and literature until I found myself on the professor's side of a desk at a university.

Long before that happened, the family home was sold, and until I purchased the house I now live in, I shared trees with the city or neighbors or campuses where I have taught. And since my life has been evenly split between residence in the Northeast and Northwest, I have lived always among trees, even if I didn't own them. There are those who love the expanse of Midwest plains or deserts or seascapes, but much as I might enjoy them for a short while, I feel uncomfortable in a place without trees. Even as I write this, a tall linden shades my study window, the window I have looked through more than any other. I watch from a height I would never dare climb to.

At the midpoint in what will probably be my allotted years, I purchased a house in a section of Portland that was developed around the time of the First World War. This house has become the house my children will associate with their childhood, and it became mine because its disrepair made it affordable, despite its size, even for an underpaid young professor. And it had a tree in the back yard. Most of the houses in the neighborhood do, usually a fruit tree or chestnut. Mine is a pear tree.

My pear's trunk is over sixty inches around, and I have

reached an age where I have a great deal of respect for age. But back when the tree and I were younger, possession itself was satisfaction enough. Though in my own defense, I must say that I have been generous in sharing this possession. I don't spray, so an array of insects harvests most of its bountiful but not especially tasty fruit. Sparrows and robins nest in it. Early on I built a platform reached by ladder, and my children, one after the other, have claimed it as their house. And it was. And so I have had a pear tree with three children instead of a partridge.

Those children have pretty much left the nest, but the old platform remains. I store my fireplace logs under it, and on the weathered two-by-sixes where my children played I keep a couple of large, shallow bowls where birds splash as I read in the dappled light of late summer afternoons. There is no returning to the time when my children played among the pear's branches, or further back to the trees that I've associated with the Eden of my own childhood. The biblical paradise and the remembered splendor of a childhood may both be mythic, the imagery of poetry. But poems spring from reality.

The first great poem nearly begins with "trees bearing fruit with their seed inside in their several kinds. God saw that it was good." And so must I in my backyard sitting under my pear tree, while the summer light paints the rooftops and fences of the neighborhood as an old master might. For a fleeting moment the world has the look and feel of paradise (or of childhood). Only a fool would let the moment escape. Fleeting as it is, the moment is as real as the tree that bends over me and is, in its own way, the gift of a true love.

Reading Women

I 'VE CAST OVER my first childhood home in the Berkshire hills an Edenic glow, and I suppose my personal myth is so strong because I did not outgrow that garden but left it. My family moved from that country town to a large city just before my teens. My father had no choice, but in my mind it was an unforgivable tragedy: being cast from the Garden of Eden. I hated the city, didn't fit in, and grew homesick for our old home. I moped and grumped until my desperate mother, burdened enough with her own adjustments and my two younger brothers, shipped me off to an aunt who was my Godmother and who lived in a small triangular house with walls of glass that looked out on wooded lots. So ended what promised to be the summer of my discontent.

Uncle Jack sold insurance in New York City and drove home to the country only on the weekends. My much older cousin was in the Air Force. It was just "me and Aunt Ruth." She brooked no moping or grumping. And no TV until it was dark outside. It had been years since Ruth had a child in her home, so her brand of fairy-godmothering was to treat me pretty much as an equal. When we weren't

The Play of Light

doing our chores or exploring the woods, there were books. My uncle and aunt were old-fashioned readers, omnivorous and insatiable when it came to books. They had just finished *Dr. Zhivago,* which had only recently been published in America. It was a big book, bigger in ways that I could hardly imagine at the time, but I picked it up, turned to the first page, and began reading about the boy "who covered his face with his hands and burst into sobs." I read on to the second chapter, "A Girl from a Different World." The girl was the sixteen-year-old Larisa Feodorovna Guishar, Zhivago's Lara, and my Lara. I was smitten and read on and on.

When darkness fell, and we had finished the dishes, Aunt Ruth and I began what became an evening ritual of reading and of leaping up periodically to watch long-horned beetles or giant moths drawn from the dark woods to the glass walls. Pale green Luna moths floated from the soft shadows like the ghosts of woodland fairies. As I read of snow glistening on Moscow streets, fireflies flashed beyond my reflection in the window. Lara grew older as the summer passed away and so did I.

With her reading glasses at the edge of her nose, my aunt studied a book by Adele Davis, a rather radical nutritionist of the fifties whom my uncle dismissed as a health nut. As my aunt's equal, I suffered through breakfasts with brewer's yeast on my cereal and all manner of unsavory but wholesome diets. On the weekends my uncle, who was a chops-and-steak man, placed a ban on all things healthy—I even got to sip from his beer when we watched the Friday-night boxing matches. But all the weekdays, I lived in my aunt's world, a woman's world at that, and one that I had not really shared before, or would again until I married. Yet it was not my mother's world. Aunt Ruth "cultivated" only wildflowers, which I helped her transplant. She and my uncle sang in a music group, and in a lovely soprano would sing to herself when I was out of her sight. She read *The Catholic Worker*, bought food at a co-op, allowed me to go to Temple with the nearest neighbor boy, and shared hospitality with the first black people I ever saw up close.

We took trips into the city sometimes with my uncle, often to spend a day in the Museum of Natural History. We walked through the Hall of Man one afternoon and carefully examined the case that detailed the growth of the human embryo, Aunt Ruth reading in her matter-of-fact tone the process of conception and birth. And she told me how she had lost several children. "Just that size," she said, pointing to the cross-sectioned model in the display case. She was lucky to have had my cousin. Imagining that uterus inside my aunt gave me a shudder of pity and a confusing sense of awe that only years later would I begin to appreciate, and have never really understood.

So when Lara and Zhivago fell in love and had a child and suffered, as adults must, I probably read beyond my years those August nights. By the end of the summer, I was still a boy but Lara was a woman my aunt's age, and I loved both of them. I finished my first big book, packed my insect collection, and returned to a home that I now missed. But even as I waved goodbye to Aunt Ruth from the train, I was planning the next summer.

There were to be three more, all wonderful in their way, but none quite like the first. I became a full-fledged teenager with summer jobs and girlfriends, misguidedly putting aside the things that I associated with childhood. My world and my aunt's grew far apart. In my last year of high school, an aggressive cancer took my aunt suddenly despite all her years of healthy living. My painful regret was that I never told her how much I cared. So much became clear with loss. I remembered then the little boy in the novel who covered his face and cried and who would grow up to love Lara. Much later I would remember the little boy I was, reading into the summer nights with Ruth.

I know more now. I know my mother took in my cousin, Ruth's only child, when they lived in New York City and he was getting into trouble. I know now that my mother's sending me may have been as much a gift to my aunt as it was to me. I filled the summers for an eccentric and lovely woman struggling in a lonely and difficult marriage. Nothing was as simple as it seemed. Both women knew that and gave me the freedom to read and reread as deeply as I could.

Reading by Heart

I N T H E S H O E B O X E S of photographs that serve as our family archive, my mother and aunt look into the camera over years when they were younger than I am now. In a favorite photo, my brother and I sit with my mother in a padded winged armchair. My brother is perhaps two and seated on my mother's lap; I, perhaps five, am pleasantly squeezed next to her. We share a book, and my brother is turning a page. It is very much the kind of picture my father loved to take, for it captured how he wished to see his family: his wife as mother reading to her children; his Madonna with Children and Book.

Yet it was an accurate portrait. Mother read to us, and her voice is often the voice I hear in my mind when I read. She brought me out into her gardens and she carried me into the world of words. Reading and reading aloud trigger all sorts of remembrances, of my childhood and of my children's.

A summer ago, through the downstairs hall flowed the sound of my recently graduated daughter reading the latest adventures of Harry Potter to my wife. Her voice came to me slightly muted by intervening rooms, more melody

The Play of Light

than words and sentences. I knew the rising and falling notes well, knew them from years and years ago.

As a child this daughter would sing herself back to sleep if she awoke after we tucked her in. Sitting alone some nights, I would by chance hear her song as it floated gently and almost inaudibly down the wooden hill of stairs. And in those days if I imagined the song of angels that was the sound I thought I heard. Only once did I intrude close enough to hear the words: that night Christmas carols, or the parts of them she remembered, spliced in perfect harmony.

Throughout my daughter's life, we have had a succession of schnauzers that inevitably are by her side in family albums. And in one of the albums, or perhaps just in my memory, the three-year-old sits at the bottom of our porch stairs pretend-reading to one of those schnauzers who snuggles next to her and eyes her knowingly. She told the story as she remembered my wife or me reading it to her. She read it by heart.

At bedtime I read to this daughter as I did to the older brother and sister who listened before her, and at some point she inveigled me to add short made-up stories to the menu. Looking back these may have been among the quietest and happiest minutes in my life; only further back, snuggled in my own childhood bed listening to my mother or father in the near dark, do I find equal treasure.

A lifetime becomes a kind of library with each year adding a shelf of new acquisitions. A chronological catalogue might make an interesting index to anyone's life. And like other memories the early ones imprint deeply and persist as intervening years confuse the record of middle age. One of the unexpected joys of parenthood may be reentering those old books in the company of a child whose pleasure and willingness to be carried away are infectious.

I think of those first listens and reads as nighttime activities, the story or rhymes a narrow bridge between the real world and an imaginative one, between wakefulness and dream. The stuff of reading, like a magic gift in a fairy tale, works a spell, slowly. But inevitably it opens our awareness and propels us on to adulthood. It leads us out of ourselves. And yet its path is rarely straightway, and in its crookedness it reveals not only what the literal minded would call the real world but also the world of fantasy, make-believe, and imagination.

I do not recall when I began to read myself to sleep or when my wife and I let our children tuck themselves in. Perhaps it was like so many other passages that evade trauma or drama, paths that do not reveal themselves until they are well trod. Illness, nightmares, sorrow, and, once when I was a boy, a guilty conscience: only these could bring a parent back to the bedside, book in hand.

Accurately or not I link the reading-aloud habit with trips to the library: I well remember my first card, and my glee in first carting home the maximum number of library books possible. I think of the entitlement cards I've carried in my wallet: library card, driver's license, draft card, voting card, credit cards. My worn library card may have carried me further and given me more than any of the others.

My daughter reads Harry Potter to my wife for the fun of it, relishing I believe the reversal of roles. My brothers and I read to my parents in their last days, the roles also reversed. I have no idea where our voices or the words we read took my parents. Did it take them back? Did they dream ahead to a better place without regret or pain? What was in their hearts? Unanswerable questions, perhaps. Asking someone to read to you seems very much like asking someone to remember you in his or her prayers.

I heard the poet William Stafford once say that he would give up all he had ever written to write something new, to go through the adventure one more time. This is as true of reading as it is of writing, for reading is a most civilized act—the one act of greed with high moral value. Often I have stretched out a good book anticipating the pleasure of one more chapter or reread old favorites known by heart. These are pleasures I hope to enjoy for the rest of my life, the pleasures of traveling with good books between the waking world and whatever sleep befalls me.

Circles of Love

O N ONE of the summer nights after hearing my
daughter read to my wife, I taught a small class in a
room with a wall of windows—a room with a view. Seated
with my students in an irregular circle, I could watch through
those windows the light of the setting sun on the campus
theater, or catch bright glints playing over the five bronze
statues in the center of the little quadrangle outside.

As is so often the case in summer, my class was, in the
parlance of our time, "diverse"—wonderfully so. One of
the men brought his ten-year-old son. One of the women
brought her daughter, a baby of eight weeks, the youngest
student ever to endure my lectures.

When the baby and the boy joined us, our seminar circle
mirrored the circle of statues just beyond our window, as
if the groups were reflections of each other, caught on the
surface of still pools. When the baby occasionally drew the
class's attention away from our discussion of literature and
nature, I would look out the window, as her mother settled
her, and wonder which circle was the reflection.

Four of the statues sit comfortably on rocks, just as my
students would sit comfortably, if I gave in to their pleas

to hold class outside. The fifth statue, a young child, plays on the ground at the feet of a bearded Christ, evidently early in his ministry—Christ the teacher. Two adults, a man and a woman, are looking at the face of Christ. Christ and a second woman, perhaps the mother of the child, watch the toddler, who is seated and reaching for something: leaf, bug, dandelion, pebble? I noticed that a gust of wind sometimes obliged the bronze child with the gift of a real leaf.

I have seen many representations of Christ the teacher over the years, but I confess they have impressed me vaguely at best. And I have spent a life moving through rooms where crucifixes are hung, but they are so familiar that I am usually aware only of their absence. But the statues, bulky and bronze, move me—not to Calvary or the crucifixion, but to Christmas, to the manger.

Christ is center of that circle, too, and of that season, so different from the rest of the year. I remember peering into the miniature stable that housed our manger and the statues of the Holy Family, the Magi, the shepherds, an angel or two, and my favorites: the sheep, the donkey, the cow, the horse, and one camel.

As I sat cross-legged, arranging the figurines according to my notion of how the scene unfolded, I believe I entertained my first sustained thoughts about God. This was long before I had a sense of belonging to a religion, long before I realized there might be other religions, other beliefs— although certainly my parents took me to church, and certainly I bowed my head with Mother at night in prayer.

My first notions of God, there by the manger, persisted for a long time; perhaps I have never given them up entirely. Untroubled then by doctrine, or questions of historical accuracy, I was drawn naturally to the folk traditions in which kings and shepherds and animals share not so much a moment of adoration but one of love. I was a country boy who lived in town, so my ideas of animals were no better informed than my images of farmers, angels, and kings, and to see them all as witnesses circled around the smaller circle of the Holy Family seemed right. And at the time I saw the circles in the manger from inside the circle of my own family—as secure as I ever would be.

Later the realities of my religion, and the realization that there were other religions, would expand, refine, conflict with, and confuse my first simple ideas of God. Early on I took it for granted that my neighbors of other faiths attended churches of other names but pretty much thought what we thought. But I would discover that in my own religion alone, views diverged widely on issues small and large. I have spent a life walking through halls of learning with priests, many of them theologians and philosophers, all of them teachers in a line that one might trace back to the rabbi in Galilee, He who said, "Let the little children come to me," and even my friends the priests do not always see eye to eye, and many of them holy men. So I wonder how the ideas of God and religion grow within us, how they may converge or separate as we think and feel our way through a life.

Ask a friend to remember when she first had an idea of God—not whether she believed, but when she first considered the possibility. Watch her silently work back through a tangle of thoughts and feelings. Listen to her story. Invariably the journey back simplifies. I believe the pull of those first felt thoughts is away from the complex, and beyond dogma. Pain, sorrow, old age, death—the tests of faith—invite the simplest cries from the heart: *Be with me. Help me. Mother. Father. Child. God.* In the circles of crying-out and listening are the lessons of love; and what we hear and say echoes voices before us, around us—perhaps, beyond us.

The Play of Light: An Epilogue

The sight of the star filled them with indescribable joy.

MATTHEW 2:10

O N THE SECOND of October, the night of the full moon, I watched the reflected sunset on the glass of the city's tallest buildings. With perhaps a hundred other like-minded people, I joined in a Moonviewing—an annual tradition held in the Japanese Garden that overlooks Portland's eastern reach toward Mt. Hood.

Even in early autumn after the driest of years, snow flanked the mountain in broad patches that took the pastel pinks and purples of the dimming light. The sunset, the mountain faded away; the city lights began to flicker. In less than twenty minutes, the moon rose over the silhouetted outline of the Cascades.

For centuries, Japanese poets have looked at similar sights, and ancient woodcuts capture a kindred moon above a Mt. Fuji that looks very much like the mountain before me. Steeped as they were in Zen, the classic poets could suggest in a common sight a link to something greater. And sitting in a Japanese garden where paper lanterns lit the pathway, it was tempting to seek the transcendental. Yet the poem that came to mind was quite mundane:

Lovely moon on high—
but when the clouds obscure it
necks enjoy the rest.

In this brief haiku, nearly four centuries ago, Basho caught for me the intriguing delight of the play of light that can be taken for granted or elevated to esthetic or spiritual heights, though at the risk of a sore neck.

I had hoped, actually, to crane my own neck at the end of the month to see a blue moon, a second full moon in the same month. I suppose the second full moon would have looked just like the first, but there was something fascinating about a celestial oddity. Again Basho's poem came to mind, for not only clouds, but rain also closed the month. No moon then on Halloween, just the reflections of masquerading streetlights in the black puddles. Most of the porch lights were off, and instead, the neighbors set out carved pumpkins with candles, and up and down the street the beams of parent-held flashlights led costumed children to their tricks and treats.

I tried to see the world as I saw it myself through a Halloween mask, breathing in my own breath and ignoring as best I could the black elastic string my mother had knotted to keep the mask snug on my face. The eyeholes framed a scene not quite as dazzling as Christmas but one splendid and safely spooky: the madly grinning pumpkins, the frightening visages of the older kids, and the slices of homes lit beyond the half-opened doors: corners of easy chairs, refrigerator doors, tables not quite cleared of supper dishes. And the spell and magic of it all grew out of lights set against the dark night.

I find it hard to avoid the spell of the night sky and whatever signs it may offer. And in this, I am guilty of not practicing what I teach. In my poetry classes, I am forever chiding my students for reaching for the symbolic and reading between the lines. Yet, give me light in the sky, and I am quite ready to leap beyond the text. It is not, usually, a leap into insight or answers so much as a leap into awkwardly phrased and sometimes haunting questions. Most likely, I am often looking in when I suppose I am looking up.

I expected such questions when the Leonid meteor shower rained over Oregon in the middle of November. But when the day came, so did Oregon rain. The weatherman was not encouraging, so I did not set my alarm for two in the morning, when the viewing would have been best if the sky were clear. I woke at two anyway; it was not raining and I couldn't tell how heavy the clouds were from my window. On tiptoes, lest I wake my sleeping family, I bundled against the cold, and in floppy watch cap climbed a ladder to the flat part of my roof. I climbed twice: once to bring up a cup of tea, the second time, a lawn chair. In silhouette, I was Santa, but a couple of months early. The neighbors were all asleep below me. With lawn chair as bed and sky as ceiling, I reclined into the night, waiting and watching. For what?

I remembered that when the comet Hale-Bopp hung above the top of our lilac tree, I insisted that my wife join me on our back stairs to watch. It was just a white blur on the sky that reminded me of an eraser smudge on a chalky blackboard. That blur, like so much in the night sky, humbles a human—our light burns so shortly in the small lanterns of single lives. Yet I could tell my wife that in all of time, no human had ever stood where we were

The Play of Light

and watched the comet. Our witness seemed important, if only as an assertion of our unique moment in the face of the universe's dark immensity.

I remembered a July fifth, when the morning paper informed me that three planets would be visible that night. When it was dark, my two daughters joined me in our blacktop street to find an opening in the trees where we tried to spy Venus, Mars, and Jupiter. At our feet were scattered remains from the neighborhood fireworks that had blazed like shooting stars the night before. What great forces brought those heavenly bodies into their celestial triangle? And what force conspired to create our familial triangle? By August the planets would move apart to wander in their mindless orbits, but we would remember standing close together on a summer night under a providential sky.

So in November, I craned my neck again looking for lights. They came like raindrops, almost imperceptible at first, and then every thirty, every ten seconds. It was like charting the contractions before a birth as each bright burst rent the sky. I grew greedy for more and watched until my eyes watered. I lost count of meteors but did the math of my life. Leonid will shower the world again in 2032. I would be ninety. The odds of my seeing them again were not good.

Was it enough just to see on that one night all those lights that had traveled so far, so long? Basho would have said yes. But I grew cold, and my neck was sore. In the distance I could hear sirens—a crime, a fire, an accident? An owl crossed the moon. Most of the world slept, and no one saw me climb the ladder from the roof like a disappointed Magus seeking a Savior, or a cat burglar still ready to steal more epiphanies from other night skies.

The Play of Light

Acknowledgments

W ITH THANKS, I look East to Michael Wilt and the good folks at Cowley who helped me weave together this little book. And in the Northwest I thank my friend Brian Doyle, who has encouraged this old writer to keep the faith. I am indebted also to my young friend Gina Agosta, who assisted with the technical preparation of the manuscript. Marlene Moore, dean at the University of Portland, and Brother Donald Stabrowski, provost, gave me both time and kind words when I need them most. I thank them. I thank Bruna Della Gasperina for her stories and the glasses of wine. So much of this book grew out of my life with my family, and I am forever grateful.